Lee Cummings has written a modern-day instruction manual for an authentic and powerful Christian life. The stories are fun, the history lessons are great, and the book itself is very practical, but what I appreciate most is the way Lee inspires us to live all out and be the light we are meant to be!

—JOHN VEREECKEN
FOUNDER, VIDA INTERNACIONAL, SALTILLO, MEXICO
PRESIDENT, LIDERE
AUTHOR, *CORAZÓN DE CAMPEON*

Lee Cummings has written a compelling challenge to the church to rise up to its calling. *Be Radiant* will encourage each reader as they pursue what it means to be kingdom light to their own world. This truly is fuel for the soul!

—MARK BATTERSON
LEAD PASTOR, NATIONAL COMMUNITY CHURCH
AUTHOR, *IN A PIT WITH A LION ON A SNOWY DAY*
AND *THE CIRCLE MAKER*

As a father of three I have observed how normal it is for small children to be afraid of the dark. I have seen the same behavior in the body of Christ over thirty-five years of ministry—it's a sign of our immaturity as Christians always motivated by the fear of darkness missing our eternal purpose. I am excited to see the Lord raising up a generation of leaders such as Lee Cummings who are encouraging the body to rise above the fear of the times and take their light into the places of darkness as His messengers!

—LOREN COVARRUBIAS
OVERSEER, MT. ZION, CLARKSTON, MI
HOST, *IT'S A NEW DAY!*

Lee is a prophetic voice to the local church in a time when we all need clarity and candor. This book will

challenge all of us to be the light our dark world so desperately needs.

—BRADY BOYD

SENIOR PASTOR, NEW LIFE CHURCH

AUTHOR, *SONS & DAUGHTERS*

This is a book that squarely addresses the big issues facing believers today. In a world engulfed with deep and growing spiritual darkness, it is time for the church to become the light Jesus commissioned us to be. This book leads us back to the biblical basics of how to do that in an inspiring and engaging manner. I love this book and highly recommend it to any believer ready to make a difference for Christ.

—JIMMY EVANS

SENIOR ELDER, TRINITY FELLOWSHIP, AMARILLO, TX

PRESIDENT, MARRIAGE TODAY

In this book Lee Cummings clearly paints the picture of the need today and our biblical responsibility to shine brightly. But we are not left there simply to be inspired—we will also be challenged to step forward to make a difference in this generation as we turn up the intensity of our light for God and His kingdom!

—TOM LANE

EXECUTIVE SENIOR PASTOR, GATEWAY CHURCH

SOUTHLAKE, TX

In *Be Radiant* Lee compels us, the church, to refocus back on the gospel and to be the light we're called to be in a rapidly deteriorating culture. He gives practical insight into taking the gospel into our fast-changing world to make a difference.

—DUANE VANDERKLOK

LEAD PASTOR, RESURRECTION LIFE CHURCH

GRANDVILLE, MI

Pastor Lee puts his thumb on our bashful, therapeutic Christianity in *Be Radiant*. I feel the "patch" of the gospel being peeled off of my soul and the eternal power of redemption coming alive in me as I read. Prepare the cabin for takeoff.

—JARED ANDERSON
WORSHIP LEADER, NEW LIFE CHURCH
FOUNDING MEMBER, DESPERATION BAND
SONGWRITER, "RESCUE" AND "GREAT I AM"

Amidst the clutter and chatter about who and what the church is, Lee Cummings emerges as a clear and challenging voice. Lee combines his years of church-planting pastoral work with his considerable reading and reflection to bring a biblically grounded, theologically rich vision of what it means to be the people of God. This book is sure to awaken the holy imagination of pastors and believers so that the light of Christ will indeed be radiant in us.

—GLENN PACKIAM
AUTHOR, *LUCKY* AND *SECONDHAND JESUS*
LEAD PASTOR, NEW LIFE DOWNTOWN

Christians don't have to apathetically await the return of Jesus. Lee challenges us to resurrect our core purpose as salt and light in a dark world. The church shouldn't run from the darkness; it must run toward the darkness and be what God has called us to be. It is possible to see the amazing happen in the most unlikely of places—any church can truly be radiant!

—NATE RUCH
PASTOR, EMMANUEL CHRISTIAN CENTER
SPRING LAKE PARK, MN

*BE RADIANT

Shine Bright!

Lea Canning

*BE RADIANT

LEE CUMMINGS

PASSIO

Most Charisma House Book Group products are available at special quantity discounts for bulk purchase for sales promotions, premiums, fund-raising, and educational needs. For details, write Charisma House Book Group, 600 Rinehart Road, Lake Mary, Florida 32746, or telephone (407) 333-0600.

Be Radiant by Lee Cummings
Published by Passio
Charisma Media/Charisma House Book Group
600 Rinehart Road
Lake Mary, Florida 32746
www.charismahouse.com

Unless otherwise noted, all Scripture quotations are from the Holy Bible, English Standard Version. Copyright © 2001 by Crossway Bibles, a division of Good News Publishers. Used by permission.

Scripture quotations marked NIV are from the Holy Bible, New International Version. Copyright © 1973, 1978, 1984, International Bible Society. Used by permission.

Scripture quotations marked NKJV are from the New King James Version of the Bible. Copyright © 1979, 1980, 1982 by Thomas Nelson, Inc., publishers. Used by permission.

Scripture quotations marked NLT are from the Holy Bible, New Living Translation, copyright © 1996, 2004, 2007. Used by permission of Tyndale House Publishers, Inc., Wheaton, IL 60189. All rights reserved.

Scripture quotations marked THE MESSAGE are from *The Message: The Bible in Contemporary English*, copyright © 1993, 1994, 1995, 1996, 2000, 2001, 2002. Used by permission of NavPress Publishing Group.

Cover design by Justin Evans
Design Director: Bill Johnson

Visit the author's website at radiantchurch.tv.

Library of Congress Control Number: 2012921684
International Standard Book Number: 978-1-62136-032-2
E-book ISBN: 978-1-62136-033-9

While the author has made every effort to provide accurate telephone numbers and Internet addresses at the time of publication, neither the publisher nor the author assumes any responsibility for errors or for changes that occur after publication.

First edition

13 14 15 16 17 — 9 8 7 6 5 4 3 2 1
Printed in the United States of America

DEDICATION

To my beloved Jane~

You have been my constant encourager and greatest partner.

Two are better than one...

CONTENTS

FOREWORD

THIS IS THE book I wish I had written! As I read through the first chapters of the book you now hold in your hands, I couldn't help but be amazed by the array of vital topics addressed in Lee Cummings's book, *Be Radiant*. In this hour when so many books are essentially fluff or rehashed messages that have already been preached or written over and over, the message of this book immediately fell across my eyes and mind as a ray from heaven. When I read a new book, I always ask myself, "How will this book stand in posterity? Is it in the category of a timeless tome, certain to affect generations? Or is it a trending book that addresses a hot topic that will quickly cool and lose significance in a number of years? Will this book have a long or short lifespan?" As I read this book, the answer to this question came quickly: this will be a long-lasting book that has the potential to guide believers for generations. In fact, as I read it, I kept thinking of great men of God from the past who wrote books that have enlightened men's minds for years. Though those authors have been in heaven for many years, their voices and the truths they proclaimed still speak through their written works. In my personal library I have one shelf where I keep such treasured books. I tell you, this book by Lee Cummings will be placed on that shelf alongside the other timeless books I treasure.

As I speak and correspond with pastors across America, I find among them a great sense of hopelessness because of the many and drastic cultural changes sweeping across every segment of society. The America many of us grew up in no longer exists, and the fragments of it that do remain are at risk under the threat of destruction. This pertains not only to secular society but also to the church itself. The church in America has so radically changed that it is now a pleasant surprise to find a congregation that attends weekly services with their Bibles. As secular society has changed, unfortunately, the church has changed with it—so much so that, in many instances, the Word of God is no longer the central focus. As a result we have large churches that are biblically illiterate. Lee writes, "Intentionally or unintentionally, we have developed great crowds but unprepared people."

One of the most disturbing signs of the church's condition in America can be witnessed every Sunday as many arrive at their local churches with no accompanying Bible. Some may claim they no longer need to carry it because scriptures are flashed onscreen for all to see. But the fact is, the role of the Bible in the life of the church and its members is diminishing. Sadly, in churches and in sermons across America, the Bible has been reduced to "a source" among many resources. Truth has been compromised to accommodate larger crowds. To avoid offending the people who attend but aren't deeply committed—or to avoid taking a public stand that could jeopardize the church's or a ministry's IRS status—many church leaders have opted to steer clear of strong positions on moral issues, avoiding their God-given responsibility to speak the truth.

Lee writes, "The American church is dangerously close to becoming marginalized, not because the gospel is any less effective than it ever has been, but because we have lost focus of what that gospel really is and our responsibility to carry it. We have subtly transformed the gospel of Jesus Christ into a 'self-help' message of therapy for your soul, literally a way to enhance your already good life."

He rightly tells us, "We do not have any lack of Bibles or

biblical knowledge. We have more resources, television programs, and bookstores than at any other time in history. We have hundreds of translations of the Bible available to us, and the Internet has made lack of information a relic of the past."

Lee reminds us, "The Word of God has been the centering source of stability from the very beginning. In the midst of intense persecution and growing challenges, the church constantly stayed rooted and focused by returning to the Scriptures." He continues to warn us that with "so many alternative voices...bombarding our minds, without a strong foundation in the Word of God, we will lose our equilibrium."

Losing our equilibrium is precisely what is happening, and it is exactly the reason why this book is so vital for you to read. As Lee states, "While it is true that we have more access and availability to the Bible and biblical resources than ever before, ironically...[we have] an epidemic of biblical illiteracy within the church."

What we know affects our convictions and the way we choose to live our lives. When the Bible is marginalized and when absolutes are thrown to the wind, the church differs very little from the world we have been sent to influence. Lee presents the startling report, "All of the current polls and studies confirm that evangelical Christians are divorcing at the same rate as those in the world, participating in premarital sex at the same rate, and are in the same amount of debt as those who are outside the church. There are serious problems facing the church."

Lee speaks as a prophet of old when he says, "The church has been described as a thermometer instead of a thermostat. We are no longer setting the spiritual temperature of culture; we are now merely registering the temperature of the world around us."

Though these statements are not true of every church, the general condition of the church has morally declined. Although it is televised and marketed to the masses, the spiritual power and spiritual gifts reflected in the church have dwindled until they are completely absent in many churches. Those churches that once allowed the power and presence of the Holy Spirit to manifest notably in their midst have so changed that it is possible for a person in sin to attend church, be uplifted by positive messages, and yet remain unchallenged and unchanged by those messages. This is why it is essential we hear what the Holy Spirit is saying and to allow Him to renew us with a new passion for Christ and a call to holiness. This foreword is not intended to be a doomsday interpretation of the present, but a call—along with Lee's own pleadings—for the church to rise, shine, and *be radiant!*

Lee profoundly reminds us that *light shines best in darkness.* Christ called us to be lamps to bring light to the world (Matt. 5:14–16). Lamps were made for dark rooms, and they are intended to shine and give light and definition to those who couldn't see clearly because of the darkness. If we will embrace our true identity as *the* church and do what God intended for us to do—to live fueled by the power of the Holy Spirit and to give witness to the truth—this could indeed be our greatest hour. Lee boldly tells us, "This is not the time in history for us to pull up, pull back, or pull out. This is the hour for the church to arise. This is the time to fill your lamp with oil of passion for Jesus and His glorious cause and to rush headlong into the fray."

Rushing headlong into the fray is what you and I *must* do. This is a time for us to say, "Yes, Lord, we are here! Use us!" This is a unique moment when God is calling us to lift the light of His Word and let it shine in a world that will otherwise become completely darkened. And if we will hearken to what the Spirit is saying, and then do what He has called us to do, we will find that this *is* our time to shine and to shine brightly. But it is imperative for us to hear Lee's cry to us that "without a renewed sense of open arms to the Holy Spirit, there is no possibility that the church can possibly navigate the waters of a world in turmoil." However, if we are filled with the Spirit, and if we give the Word of God a central, unmitigated position of authority in our lives, the power of the Holy Spirit will move—and we will "leave our fingerprints" all over this generation. *Yes, Lord!*

I have tried to write a book such as this, but at this time the Holy Spirit has used Lee Cummings to state these urgent truths in unequivocal terms. I am so thankful to God for breathing upon him to put these truths into print.

Please take time to read this book. *Read it intently.* Let the Holy Spirit challenge you, convict you, and change you. I testify that I have personally been challenged as I've read *Be Radiant.* And when you are finished reading it, don't let it become merely another book on your bookshelf. Let this book be the beginning of a new heart cry from your spirit for a fresh infilling of the Spirit's oil. For surely God is calling you, me, and all of His people in these times to *be radiant!*

—RICK RENNER

AUTHOR OF *SPARKLING GEMS* AND *A LIGHT IN DARKNESS*

FOUNDING SENIOR PASTOR OF MOSCOW GOOD NEWS CHURCH

LET THERE BE LIGHT

THIS BOOK IS an invitation, an invitation to take a look in the mirror at ourselves.

Mirrors are nothing new to us. They form part of our most basic daily ritual that we repeat often each day throughout all of the days of our lives. We use the mirror to reflect and reevaluate the appearance of things and make corrections as needed. We know how we can look and should look, but we are also not ignorant of the fact that throughout the day, and across even larger spans of time, things get out of sorts. That look in the mirror helps us to see how things currently stand and to walk away looking our best, filled with confidence.

As those who have been called to be the light of the world, we need to take a good look at ourselves. Are we shining as brightly as we can, or has the light that once burned bright begun to grow dim? Have we grasped the revelation that each of us has been placed by God specifically where He wants us, or have we allowed our passion to wane and our sense of purpose to be hidden under a bushel by the enemy of our soul? These are important and vital questions to ask ourselves.

In order to make an honest assessment of each of our own lives, we must not merely evaluate ourselves by comparison to one another. We need a standard that is higher and a promise that accurately and honestly portrays our ultimate calling and potential as God's light in the midst of a world gone dark. Throughout the pages of Scripture God has laid out an eternal purpose and a pattern from cover to cover that illustrates what it means to be His radiant people. What I have attempted to do is lay out a sketch of what you were always meant to look like and the vocation to which God has called you to, even before the foundations of the world.

My hope is that as you read the following pages, these ideas will not be read as an indictment as much as an inspiration to the body of Christ to move out from behind the winepress of intimidation and fear and arise. The world is desperately waiting to see the glory and the beauty of our God. Darkness is occupying territory that was meant to be filled with the truth and light. It's time for you and me to see ourselves for who we really are in Christ.

I pray that as you look into this blurry mirror of words that I have used to articulate these truths to the best of my ability, somehow you will see the glorious face of your Savior smiling back at you and speaking your name and calling you to boldly and courageously shine!

Chapter 1

ARISE, SHINE!

Arise, shine, for your light has come, and the glory of the LORD has risen upon you. For behold, darkness shall cover the earth, and thick darkness the peoples; but the LORD will arise upon you, and his glory will be seen upon you. And nations shall come to your light, and kings to the brightness of your rising.

—ISAIAH 60:1–3

THOMAS EDISON DID not invent the lightbulb. I know that may come as a surprise to you, but it's true.

Contrary to what you may have been taught as a child in school or read in a trivia book, there were several other inventors who came before him—such men as Allesandro Volta and Joseph Swan to name just a few, as well as many others you and I will never hear about who worked tirelessly over decades in an attempt to invent and develop an electric-powered lightbulb.

There were several challenges that made it difficult to develop a simple and reproducible lightbulb that was cost effective and reliable. There were even more questions about how it could be put into practical use once such a lightbulb was finally refined and capable of being manufactured. The electrical grids and power outlets we are so accustomed to now that power our homes and neighborhoods were still a distant dream of the futurists. Enter Edison.

Thomas Edison was one of America's finest minds and most prolific inventors of his generation. Nicknamed the

"Wizard of Menlo Park," where he resided and invented in his state of New Jersey, Edison would have more than one thousand patents registered in his name before the end of his life. Most of his inventions were focused around mass communications, things such as the phonograph and the first motion picture camera. But the long struggle to develop sustainable, electric lighting for the masses intrigued him and drove him to place all his focus on this one project.

It was much more than just a science project to him. He believed the lightbulb was the linchpin to making a dramatic jump forward as a civilization. Everything else would change once the lights were turned on, so to speak. Manufacturing, travel, and the formation of communities and neighborhoods would literally reshape culture as it was becoming more "enlightened."

His ambition and vision led him to gather all the research both current and from the past and examine its strengths and weakness and begin from that starting point.

Combining his genius intellect and ability to see what others were unable to see about the future and an unending work ethic, Edison was able to build upon the success and failures of other researchers and their core ideas. Some of these ideas had been around for more than sixty years but yet were unresolved and undeveloped. Instead of a fragile lightbulb that would burn inconsistently and uncontrollably for a few moments before burning out or exploding, he found a new way to control the electrical current flowing into the lamp by changing the internal filament material and internal pressure, causing it to glow consistently and steadily for more than thirteen and a half hours! I think we all have heard the stories of his failures but also of his perseverance despite how many setbacks he faced. Thousands of times he failed, made adjustments, fine-tuned, and retested.

And thousands of times it didn't work the way he knew it could and eventually would.

In the end Edison and his team were able to achieve not only the creation of a lightbulb but also a lightbulb that was long lasting, dependable, and could be mass produced and sold commercially to homes and businesses. This is something no one else had been able to do. He was able to take it out of the laboratory where it was just a theory and experimental and bring it to market where it would eventually spread as a wildfire across the American landscape. He took the complex and unattainable and made it simple and practical.

Within a few short years the entire way of life in America had been completely altered. Homes, businesses, and streets were lit up long after dark. Power lines criss-crossed throughout neighborhoods, down streets, and across fields, connecting households and businesses to the energy source that would promise to make us by far a more luminous people and take our ability to fill our lives with light to a whole new level. Thomas Edison had been right. It was possible to harness the power of electricity to create a brighter future. It was possible to solve the problems that had stumped inventors and innovators of the past. Their theories could be simplified and resolved and built upon, and the world could take a drastic leap into the future.

What if we were to have our own "Edison" moment? A moment in time when we too were able to take what has to this moment been mostly theory and move it forward to action. To take all that we have believed intellectually and discover a way to go public with it. We know that Jesus said, "You are the light of the world" (Matt. 5:14), but have we known what to do with that? Theologians and religious experts have dissected that statement and hypothesized about what it means. What we haven't done well is take it from the laboratory out into the marketplace. As Thomas Edison was able to mainstream the idea of an incandescent lightbulb, so the church must find a way to mainstream grace and truth. We need this moment—the world awaits this moment.

What would that mean for the church at large? Could we become so captivated with a vision of how things could be, even should be and must be? A moment in which all of the pieces finally fell into place and all that we have known and heard about the kingdom of God and the purpose of God for our lives all came into alignment and what was left was an undying passion to do something about it?

What if we were to find that in the middle of God's big story we found where our story fits? And what would happen if we collectively, as the church, moved beyond all of the complex arguments and debates about how dark the world is and why it is the way it is and came to a realization that in large part it is that way because we as the church are not the way we are supposed to be either? Would it be liberating? More importantly would we be willing to do something about it and take a new direction into the future?

I want to cast a compelling vision for you of this new day—a day in which the light of God's glory that is deposited in the earthen vessel of every believer is suddenly released through us—a day in which the church finally realizes that the opportunity to partner with God in His kingdom agenda and all the power of His supply is greater than the darkness that stands to hold us back, blind our eyes, and cause us to abandon hope. This new day is a day to arise and shine!

I believe the church is the linchpin to everything else God wants to accomplish in our world. If we will allow Him to refine and recalibrate our understanding, I believe we can truly become who we have always been destined to be: the light of the world! But in order for God to make His church a better lightbulb, one that can finally move out of the laboratory and be ready for mass distribution, we are going to have to adjust our paradigms and fine-tune our understanding about what it means to truly *be radiant!*

THIS PRESENT DARKNESS

Every time I fly at night, I love to look down out of the small window of the airplane upon our descent at the city below and see it radiating with light, life, and constant activity, cars moving as bright little blips making their way through the electric avenues and the bright grids of neighborhoods outlined in light against the contrasting darkness of the night. It is a breathtaking reminder to me of how quickly things can change in a very short period of time. Those things that were once impossibilities have now become reality.

The world we live in is still a very dark place. Just because we have created a way to provide artificial light to cities, homes, streets, and beyond has not changed the fact that beyond the veil of what is seen is still an insidious force the Bible describes as "darkness" in this present age.

This spiritual darkness is everywhere and can even be tangibly felt at times. I have traveled to many places around the world and had moments when I sensed, in a very real way, the heaviness that comes with the presence of spiritual wickedness. I have sensed it in the Hindu temples of India, the streets of communist nations, and the halls of high academia. I have felt it perhaps most strongly in my own city, as I have driven around the city limits praying for God to move. In those moments I have sensed the darkness and seen evidence of it in the eyes and on the countenance of the people weighed down by the glum of spiritual hopelessness.

> For we do not wrestle against flesh and blood, but against rulers, against authorities, against cosmic

powers over this present darkness, against the spiritual forces of evil in the heavenly places.

—EPHESIANS 6:12

I remember when I was a brand-new believer, in my early teens, my youth pastor recommended a new book for all of us to read called *This Present Darkness*. The premise of this fictional book was that there is a spiritual battle taking place all around us between the forces of light and the forces of darkness. Frank Peretti, its author, used his storytelling skills to pull back the veil between the spiritual and natural world and show the interaction of angels and demons upon the events of everyday life in a small church in a small town. He was able to show how the smallest actions have an impact upon the spiritual climate of a community.[1]

I literally read the entire book in one sitting because I could not set it down. I was absolutely glued to it. It was the first time I had ever really given any thought to the reality of the conflict between the dark forces of wickedness and the kingdom of God. From that time forward my entire perspective about being a Christian changed. My prayer habit became a prayer life. My Bible-reading plan became a Bible-reading obsession. As I walked through the hallways of my school, I was captivated by the thought that in these very hallways spiritual warfare was taking place.

I understood for the first time that my place was to be a bright light in this very dark place.

I wish every believer could have a moment in which they could see beyond what is seeable just long enough to catch a glimpse of what is taking place within the realm of the spirit and how that is affecting and interacting with the natural course of life. It doesn't take much to see its evidences if you know what you are looking for. You just have to turn on the daily news to find evidence of this darkness's presence and dominance over the world we live in.

Its pressure and heaviness is like a heavy blanket that smothers the beauty and good out of everything and everyone. We see the shadows of it cast over our neighborhoods, schools, workplaces, families, and even our churches. Perhaps the most disturbing place we are faced with this looming darkness and dank of evil is in the piece of glass we stare into each day as we prepare to face the world we live in. I'm talking about the mirror.

Mirrors are objective in what they show us, but our eyes and the perceptions we see through are not. When we look into a mirror we aren't just seeing what is there in the raw; we are seeing ourselves through the filters of our preconceived ideas about ourselves. We too easily dismiss what we see both in the mirror and in the world as "just the way things are," without giving a second thought that things could ever be different. We see smeared across the mirror the reminder of every past failure, every disappointment, and every dream that has died unfulfilled. It's difficult enough to see ourselves there staring back at us, but even more difficult to look out beyond ourselves and see any reason to believe there is hope. Eventually our eyes adjust to the darkness, and we accept it for what it is—or what we think it is.

There is an inherent danger in creating a dualistic perspective between the supernatural and the natural world. They are not really separate as much as they are two sides to the same coin or two intricately and intertwined dimensions. If we are not careful, we can allow ourselves to separate our spiritual life from our "real" life in the way we see things. On the other hand, the benefit of such a revelation is we come to realize darkness is all around us (I would argue that often the darkness is even "within" us)—not darkness necessarily as an undefeatable force but more of a void. It is more about what is *not* there than what is there. It's the absence of light. Isn't that what darkness really is? It is those crags and crevices where light has not reached or where light has been effectively blocked out.

It is from that standpoint that we must ask ourselves the question: "What am I going to do about it?" This question is the beginning of the end for the darkness.

ISAIAH AND THE LIGHT OF NATIONS

The prophet Isaiah was a man who had experienced such a life-changing encounter as I described above. The Bible says about him that:

> In the year that King Uzziah died I saw the Lord sitting upon a throne, high and lifted up; and the train of his robe filled the temple. Above him stood the seraphim. Each had six wings; with two he covered his face, and with two he covered his feet, and with two he flew. And one called to another and said: "Holy, holy, holy is the LORD of hosts; the whole earth is full of his glory!" And the foundations of the thresholds shook at the voice of him who called, and the house was filled with smoke. And I said: "Woe is me! For I am lost; for I am a man of unclean lips, and I dwell in the midst of a people of unclean lips; for my eyes have seen the King, the LORD of hosts!"
>
> —ISAIAH 6:1–5

For one moment in time the veil between this world and the realm of the spirit was pulled back. The result for Isaiah was a change in perspective. He had come face-to-face with the almighty God of the universe and saw Him exalted and enthroned as King. For him this revelation revealed how holy and awesome God really was and also how unclean and filled with darkness he and the world were.

Isaiah was no stranger to the darker side of reality. He daily walked through the streets of Jerusalem and saw with his own two eyes how dark the times were in which he was living. He saw the evidence of darkness's influence in the wickedness and idolatry that was not just present in the pagan cultures that surrounded Judah and her borders. Every man was looking out for only his own interest. Sexual immorality, idolatry, greed, and murder were not the exception. They were now the rule. He witnessed the injustices on every level, and perhaps the darkest of all was Israel's spiritual apathy in the face of it all.

Israel was not like any other nation. They had their origin in the redemptive purposes of God. Long ago God had decided to rescue His broken and fragmented world that had descended into darkness by transgression. In His grace God had begun His redemptive plan in earnest by revealing Himself to one man by the name of Abram. We aren't exactly sure how this revelation came about, but what we are sure of is the outcome:

> Now the LORD said to Abram, "Go from your country and your kindred and your father's house to the land that I will show you. And I will make of you a great nation, and I will bless you and make your name great, so that you will be a blessing. I will bless those who bless you, and him who dishonors you I will curse, and in you all the families of the earth shall be blessed."
>
> —GENESIS 12:1–3

We know that Abram, whose name was later changed by God to Abraham (father of a multitude), believed God and left all that he was familiar with in pursuit of the place and the promise of God. That promise was given to his children and his children's children as an inheritance that made them a distinct nation. Eventually those descendants became a great nation, just as God had promised. Jacob became Israel, and his twelve children became the leaders of the twelve tribes of the nation of Israel.

The story of God's dealings with the descendants of Abraham is nothing if not a stunning picture of God's unrelenting pursuit of the heart of humanity and His commitment to His salvation plan at all cost. The Exodus story of Israel miraculously being delivered from the clutches of the Egyptian empire demonstrates that larger, grander story of a loving and jealous God who will break the dark powers of evil and rescue those who are His and bring them to Himself.

On the heels of the incredible deliverance through the Red Sea and the destruction of the Egyptian armies, God calls them to meet Him at Mount Sinai, the mountain of the Lord. It is there that God now reveals Himself and His full intentions for them as a nation:

> You yourselves have seen what I did to the Egyptians, and how I bore you on eagles' wings and brought you to myself. Now therefore, if you will indeed obey my voice and keep my covenant, you shall be my treasured possession among all peoples, for all the earth is mine; and you shall be to me a kingdom of priests and a holy nation.
>
> —EXODUS 19:4–6

It is here that God delivers to them the Ten Commandments and the Law and gives them the blueprint for designing a home for Him to dwell in their midst in a manifest and tangible way. This is now what has marked them as a special and unique nation among all the others. God, the creator of all things, now dwelt among them and spoke to them and revealed to them the Law, or the Torah, which was meant to keep them distinct and different from all the other nations of the world in the way that they lived and related to one another and the world around them.

Why was God doing all of this? It was all part of His rescue plan—to start with one man and give him a promise, to start with one family and watch them become one nation, to create His own nation out of nothing, and to reveal Himself to them and give them the vocation of being a nation of kings and priests before Him on behalf of the rest of humanity. This was Israel's calling. They were called to be a light to the nations of the world, revealing God and His glory, dispelling the darkness of ignorance and sin. God was going to "bless them," and through that blessing the Gentiles would be drawn to the goodness and superiority of their relationship with God that they too would come and seek after God as He had sought after them.

But something had gone terribly wrong. Over and over again Israel had become just as all the other nations of the world around them and forgotten their first love and their calling. They were not standing out and shining bright for all to see. They had become complacent and enslaved once again to the same darkness that shrouded the rest of the world. The remnant that God had chosen to use to bring the light of His truth and rescue had now become snared and blinded. Jerusalem—the capital city and the center of civil, economic, and spiritual life—lay in spiritual rubble and empty of any passion for the Lord, His covenant, or their calling.

This is the situation in which Isaiah comes to influence. Most scholars believe that he was most likely related to the royal family and was upper class privilege. He was intricately aware of the bleakness of the hour. There was an overwhelming sense that things were not right and that God was not pleased.

This all came to a head for him when God chose to interrupt his "normal" life and call him to be a prophetic voice to his people. God was embossing upon Isaiah's heart a vision of the greatness of God and recruiting him to call the nation of Judah back to their calling to serve as kings and priests instead of slaves and calloused carousers.

> And I heard the voice of the Lord saying, "Whom shall I send, and who will go for us?" Then I said, "Here I am! Send me."
>
> —Isaiah 6:8

Within the framework of this setting Isaiah set out to remind this nation of their destiny. They were a holy nation whom God had designated for Himself, so He could bless them and through them bring the light of salvation to the farthest reaches of the world.

> I am the Lord; I have called you in righteousness; I will take you by the hand and keep you; I will give you as a covenant for the people, a light for the nations, to open the eyes that are blind, to bring out the prisoners from the dungeon, from the prison those who sit in darkness.
>
> —Isaiah 42:6–7

Judah had become so consumed with the blessings that they forgot the purpose for their existence and for the blessing. It was all part of what God was doing to redeem and restore a broken world that lay under the sway of spiritual and moral darkness. In their prosperity they had lost their passion for God, their compassion for others, and the most prized treasure of all, their unique identity. They had forgotten who they were.

Arise! Shine!

The words of Isaiah chapter 60 are a profound prophetic call to awakening for both the nation of Judah and for you and me as the people of God today. "Arise, shine; for your light has come! And the glory the LORD is risen upon you" (v. 1, NKJV). These words carry force and are infused with holy passion. Isaiah was calling his nation to remember and return. He made it clear that darkness had indeed grown dark and that things had gotten bad but not beyond repair. God was still committed to His own purpose of rescuing and saving the world, beginning with His people, but He must first awaken them.

I believe that this message carries as much weight and glory for us today as it did the moment it was uttered thousands of years ago. We find ourselves in familiar surroundings as Isaiah had found Israel. We, the people of God, are also a holy nation and a peculiar people who have in many regards lost or forgotten our vocation. We have become mesmerized by our own obsessions, to the point of becoming numb and calloused to need around us. As Judah of old, we have lost our identity and calling along the way. In many ways the American church differs very little from the world we have been sent to. All of the current polls and studies confirm that evangelical Christians are divorcing at the same rate as those in the world, participating in premarital sex at the same rate, and are in the same amount of debt as those who are outside of the church. There are serious problems facing the church. The church has been described as a thermometer instead of a thermostat. We are no longer setting the spiritual temperature of culture; we are now merely registering the temperature of the world around us. We aren't letting our light shine as much as we are hiding it under a bushel or at worst—letting Satan blow it out. Oh, that we could get a firm understanding and renewed sense of urgency to the words of that Sunday school song!

Unfortunately we have now become known more for what we are against than what we are for—or better yet, "who" we are for. So what do we do? What is our solution? Should we run and hide, give up hope, and just come to grips with the fact that things will never change? Or is there something else?

I believe God is issuing a prophetic invitation to the church in the twenty-first century that now is the time to "arise and shine!" It is in this hour when many are willing to give up hope and abandon faith that those who have ears to hear what the Spirit is saying to the church must rise up and seize the opportunity to partner with God in what He is doing on Planet Earth. Make no mistake about it; God has not given up on His plan or His church. The church, made up of people just like you and me who are filled with the Holy Spirit, are still God's plan A. He has no plan B because the victory over the darkness has already been accomplished through the life, vicarious death, and victorious resurrection of God's own Son, Jesus Christ. He came and fulfilled all that was required to reconcile us back to God and destroy the tethers of sin and shame. Jesus came into this dark world just as we did, but instead of being overcome by the darkness, He defeated it.

> In the beginning was the Word, and the Word was with God, and the Word was God. He was in the beginning with God. All things were made through him, and without him was not any thing made that was made. In him was life, and the life was the light of men. The light shines in the darkness, and the darkness has not overcome it.
>
> —JOHN 1:1–5

God has not abandoned this world to the forces and the folly of darkness. On the contrary, He has already called light into being and set His purpose into motion, and there is no turning back. Just as Isaiah described it, "Darkness has covered the earth and gross darkness the people," but God's desire and design is to arise upon a people readied and prepared to walk in step with Him, embracing our hour of visitation and our calling. God is looking for people who can see the light shining already in their hearts and are committed to be His radiant church!

Whether you know it or not, if you identify yourself as a follower of Jesus Christ, this is what you were saved for. This is your holy calling and great inheritance—you, together with others that God has put together in this wonderful community called "the church." Not just *a* church but a church that is part of something grander: *the* church, which is His body. This has been God's intention all along: to use people just like you and me to dispel the darkness and live redemptive lives that bring healing to a blinded and broken world and to see His kingdom agenda come to bear upon the earth.

> All this energy issues from Christ: God raised him from death and set him on a throne in deep heaven, in charge of running the universe, everything from galaxies to governments, no name and no power exempt from his rule. And not just for the time being, but forever. He is in charge of it all, has the final world on everything. At the center of all this, Christ rules the church. The church, you see, is not peripheral to the world; the world is peripheral to the church. The church is Christ's body, in which he speaks and acts, by which he fills everything with his presence.
>
> —Ephesians 1:20–23, The Message

Chapter 2

ENTER THE VOID

Darkness cannot drive out darkness; only light can do that. Hate cannot drive out hate; only love can do that.

—MARTIN LUTHER KING JR.

CAN REMEMBER THAT cool, crisp September morning so well. It was the first Sunday of our new church plant, and butterflies were swarming in my gut as we drove toward our new mission frontier. Richland, Michigan, is not a large town. In fact, it's a very quaint, small bedroom community just north of the midsized city of Kalamazoo, Michigan. After months of prayer, research, and planning, today was the day when we were about to drive the stake into the ground and claim this territory for the kingdom of God. We drove down Highway 131 from Grand Rapids, which had been "home" for both Jane and me for most of our lives. As we got closer, the reality of this moment was sobering.

Months earlier I had been comfortably employed on staff at a thriving megachurch, and life seemed to be as good as it could get. Underneath the surface though I was sensing the stirring in my heart that usually shows itself when God is at work in me and preparing me for change ahead. Within the next couple months God had spoken to me about planting a church from scratch in Southwest Michigan. This was 1996, and to the best of my knowledge, church planting wasn't as trendy as it has now become. I was twenty-five, had a young family, and absolutely had no idea of how to lead a church, better yet start one. When I approached my senior pastor, instead of telling me all the reasons I shouldn't, he encouraged me and told me that this was probably the Lord. He told me he was 100 percent supportive. I will never forget his words when he told me, "Lee, you will always have a place here on staff with me, but I think you have more in you, and this will be the greatest adventure of your life."

And now it was happening. I will never forget pulling into this quiet little town very early in the morning with our red trailer (which we had named "Tabernacle One") behind our borrowed fifteen-passenger van. With our small set-up team, we were headed toward the Gull Lake Community High School. I felt as if we were a secretive team of Special Forces moving silently behind enemy lines. I felt as if we were invading enemy territory—and in fact, we were.

We set up the small sound system and the few signs we had inside the small cafetorium that had been named the Devils' Den after the school's mascot, the Blue Devils. The Devils' Den was a perfect place to hold church services and greet first-time guests. "Welcome to church!" "Welcome to the Devils' Den!" Of course this is how you start a church! Right? That day I sat in a back room with sweaty hands and a desperate heart, praying that someone would show up. At 10:00 a.m. I walked out and stood in the front row, in front of a creaky old blue plastic chair, and nodded at the volunteer worship leader to go ahead and start. Before it was all said and done, seventy people were in attendance and one person gave his heart to the Lord. I was ecstatic!

That was the beginning of an incredible journey, and it was way bigger than just starting a church. It was the genesis of a movement of people known as Radiant Church. This is a group who have wholeheartedly embraced the conviction that the church is the tip of the spear that God uses to penetrate the darkness, to enter the void, and fill the world with the light of the truth, hope of God's great salvation. Fifteen years into this journey have shaped my perspective of what darkness really is and, perhaps more importantly, how we, as the light of the world, should perceive and relate to a world gone dark and see ourselves in the midst of it all.

FIND A DARK PLACE

We desperately need to have a paradigm shift in how we see ourselves. The church must recover an aggressive sense of confidence and urgency again if we are ever going to live up to our high calling and purpose. We are not spiritually wired to live stagnant, safe lives. This will only produce bored, underdeveloped, and dissatisfied saints who learn to silence the call and replace the mission given to us by Jesus with a cheap alternative.

The American church is dangerously close to becoming marginalized, not because the gospel is any less effective than it ever has been, but because we have lost focus of what that gospel really is and our responsibility to carry it. We have subtly transformed the gospel of Jesus Christ into a "self-help" message of therapy for your soul, literally a way to enhance your already good life. The problem with this message is...well, it's not the gospel that was "once and for all delivered to the saints."

When the church forgets that its primary vocation is to be carriers of the gospel, we in reality become barriers to people seeing and hearing the gospel. Historically when the church's flame was burning brightest, there was a sense of passion and urgency to find dark places and invade them with the light of God's glory. The times in church history that we often refer to as the "Dark Ages" are marked as periods of division, corruption, and neglect of our responsibility to partner with God in His new creation work. The church by its very definition is meant to be mobilized not institutionalized.

Jesus answered him, "I will build my church, and the
gates of hell shall not prevail against it."

—MATTHEW 16:18

Gates are not offensive weapons that the enemy uses
to attack the church; they are defensive barriers that are
erected to define and defend territory possessed and controlled by the forces of hell. What did Jesus have in mind
when He made this statement? He wasn't planning for the
church to be in a stationary position. He was building the
church, made up of redeemed men and women who would
be filled with the power of the Holy Spirit and motivated to
find territory previously under the control and auspice of
the forces of darkness and overcome it. If the church is anything less than this, it ceases to be the church.

In the early twentieth century a group of radical missionaries devoted to the fulfillment of the great commission became known as One Way Missionaries. This name
is derived from their commitment to go to distant mission
fields understanding that they in all likelihood would never
return home and would most likely die a martyr's death.
One of the most famous of these pioneers was a man named
A. W. Milne. He purchased a one-way ticket to a set of small
South Pacific Islands known as the New Hebrides. After
saying his good-byes he set sail for his new home, not certain of how long he would survive but fully confident in the
call that God had placed in his heart to go and bring hope
and salvation to a people who had never heard the name
of Jesus or seen the glory of God. He was fully aware that
others who had gone before him had been killed as outsiders
and that a similar fate could await him. He went anyway.

Not only did he arrive safely, but he also lived among
the indigenous population for more than thirty-five years,
leading a majority of them to Christ and raising a family

there among them. When he died as an old man, the people he so loved buried him, celebrating his life and grieving their loss. They wrote only one statement upon his gravestone that summed up all that his life had been about and the impact he had made upon this forgotten void of a land: "When he came there was no light. When he left there was no darkness."[1]

DARKENED BELIEFS

What we believe about darkness is almost as important as what we believe about the light. So many misconceptions and false beliefs abound, and they have tainted the way we see the world and understand our mission. If we are unable to see things in the world from a kingdom vantage point, it's possible that we are trying to address issues in the dark from a matrix just as dark as the world around us. Jesus spoke passionately about this contradiction:

> Your eye is the lamp of your body. When your eye is healthy, your whole body is full of light, but when it is bad, your body is full of darkness. Therefore be careful lest the light in you be darkness. If then your whole body is full of light, having no part dark, it will be wholly bright, as when a lamp with its rays gives you light.
>
> —LUKE 11:34–36

In other words, it is possible for our "light" or our message informed by our core beliefs to become so infected with lies that it actually becomes too dull to overcome the darkness around us. How we see things matters, and it is imperative that our worldview is shaped and formed by the truth of God's Word. Could it be that some of the ineffectiveness in the body of Christ can be traced back to some of our darkened beliefs?

23

Every misconception we allow to dominate our thinking gives birth to a response just as every cause also produces a specific affect. Let's examine some misnomers and false assumptions that often keep God's people from shining as bright as we should and that steal from us our inheritance and motivation.

LIE #1: DARKNESS IS SYNONYMOUS WITH PEOPLE

Standing in line at the boarding gate of an international airport revealed to me how insidious this assumption really can be. I watch as a family of Middle Eastern descent gathered their carry-on bags and got in line to board. I watched as people looked at them suspiciously. Were they terrorists? Did they have bombs in those bags? Since 9/11 the world has become a very different place, and the way we see the world around us has lost some of its innocence. I must admit, while I stood there watching this family with two small children and a mother and grandmother boarding the plane, I found myself thinking along a similar line. I felt very uncomfortable and heard my inner dialogue going to "I sure hope I don't have to sit next to them."

A few minutes passed while I waited for my section to be called to the front of the line when I found myself arrested. Not arrested by security but by a higher authority. The Holy Spirit gripped my heart and stirred compassion for them and spoke to me very clearly. "Lee, do you not see that they are people whom I love very much? Do you think they love their children any less than you love yours? Do you think they are less valuable than you are to Me? They have dreams, hopes, fears, and a purpose for which I made them, just like I have for you."

In that moment I realized how much the darkness I feared was not external but internal. There was a void in my heart I had allowed to exist that affected the way I saw people, especially people whom the world had taught me to profile and marginalize, forgetting their humanness and uniqueness. How could I ever show the goodness of God, share the story of God, or bring light to people I viewed as "evil"? If we go back to the foundational scripture in Isaiah, we can see that the darkness affects people but is *not* people. In fact, as soon as we begin to view people as the problem, we actually become the problem.

Jesus did not see people this way. In fact, one of the aspects of His ministry that got Him into trouble with the religious establishment was that He intentionally pursued and engaged "unclean" people and brought healing, salvation, and words of hope to them. From the Samaritan woman at the well to the tax collector He called to be one of His twelve, Jesus was indeed and still is a "friend of sinners."

> The Son of Man, on the other hand, feasts and drinks, and you say, "He's a glutton and a drunkard, and a friend of tax collectors and other sinners!"
>
> —Luke 7:34, nlt

He never once excused their sin, but He excused the sinner from the bondage and blindness that controlled their lives. He brought grace and truth to their deep, dark secrets and saw the real enemy for who he was.

When we allow ourselves to buy into this belief that certain people are "clean" and others are "unclean," we become more like the Pharisees and Sadducees Jesus was conflicted with. He called them the "blind guide…the blind lead the blind" (Matt. 15:14). It is impossible to love people we have demonized. Love motivates, fear captivates, and hate stagnates. Martin Luther King Jr., the revered civil rights activist and ordained minister, said it best while facing the brutal aggression of racism tearing America apart during the 1960s:

Darkness cannot drive out darkness; only light can do that. Hate cannot drive out hate; only love can do that.[2]

If we are to overcome the gates of hell, we must start by rearranging our view of people. We can't love whom we fear, and we can't serve whom we disdain or hate. People are the victims, prisoners, and precious treasure of God's eye. To see them any other way is darkness. If our worldly trained viewpoint of people who are different than us is that they are the enemy, we will perish and fail in our assignment.

LIE #2: DARKNESS IS THE EQUAL OF LIGHT (DUALISM)

The error of dualism is a predominate belief found in most world religions. Unfortunately even Bible-believing Christians fall prey. Dualism is more or less the belief that good and evil, God and the devil, are independent—both of which are equal forces within the world.[3] This implies that the creator of the darkness of sin and evil caused by his rebellion against God is, in actuality, a force on the same level and authority as God Himself.

Too many Christians are under the impression that Satan is the polar opposite of God, equal to Him in all ways. Nothing could be further from the truth. God alone is sovereign and the eternal Creator of all things. Satan and his minions are created beings with limited power, authority, and presence. While God is all powerful (omnipotent), all knowing (omniscient), and ever present (omnipresent), Satan, angels, and demons are limited and subject to God in all things. I will argue later that not only are they subject to Jesus, but they have also been subjected to the authority of the church—the adopted children of God who are representatives of the Creator God and His kingdom.

We see all throughout the Bible that God does what He

wants and exerts His authority and power over the forces of darkness on a regular basis. Jesus demonstrated the superiority of the kingdom of God over the forces of darkness throughout His ministry by healing and delivering people from demonic control.

> And if Satan casts out Satan, he is divided against himself. How then will his kingdom stand? And if I cast out demons by Beelzebul, by whom do your sons cast them out? Therefore they will be your judges. But if it is by the Spirit of God that I cast out demons, then the kingdom of God has come upon you. Or how can someone enter a strong man's house and plunder his goods, unless he first binds the strong man?
>
> —MATTHEW 12:26–29

The redemptive work of Jesus upon the cross has in fact completely invalidated any default authority and power that Satan has possessed. Far from God's equal, darkness is used in describing this lesser kingdom and methodology because darkness is not any equal force but a weaker force. In actuality it represents a void that has yet to be filled by light. The borders of darkness are only determined by the desire and expansion of light. The cross and the resurrection of Jesus Christ have trumped the power and influence of darkness.

> He has delivered us from the domain of darkness and transferred us to the kingdom of his beloved Son, in whom we have redemption, the forgiveness of sins.
>
> —COLOSSIANS 1:13–14

In fact, the ruler of this world is only allowed to operate within certain parameters, temporarily allowed by God, in order for His purposes to be fully realized in the world. The time will come when God will ultimately make Satan and all of the other spiritual forces bow the knee to His lordship and banish them from His restored creation and glorious kingdom.

It is vital that we understand the difference. If we believe that God and Satan are equals, fear will grip our hearts and keep us from action. If the greatness of God is called into question, our perception of His glory will also be diminished. But when our hearts realize the overwhelming surety of God's plans and the strength to perform them, confidence can grow within us and propel us to reach beyond what we think is safe.

Limited by intimidation

When the devil and the powers of evil are perceived as equal in strength with God, it will inevitably produce a spirit of intimidation. When we become convinced in the power of our enemy as much as we are in the ability of God, we become unstable and fear filled. This is seen over and over within the biblical story. This spirit of intimidation is subtle, as most fear is, because it is camouflaged in "being practical" and common sense. It eats away at the foundations of our faith and confidence and affects not only how we view God but also how we ultimately view God in us. Intimidation overexaggerates our weaknesses and shrinks our view of the capacity of God.

LIE #3: DARKNESS MEANS THE END

I remember while growing up, the rule in our house was when it begins to get dark out and the streetlights come on, it's time to come home. In my mind the darker it got, the closer to the end of the day it was getting. We tend to view the spiritual condition of the world around us in this same way. How many times do we say and think to ourselves, "This world is beyond repair?" or "Things are really starting to get bad." When we hear others speak like this, we know how to interpret what is really being said: "It's getting near the end!" Evil runs rampant. Wars and rumors of wars abound. Just when you think you've seen it all, something happens so astounding, so insidious that it takes your breath away and you wonder, "How could it possibly get any worse?" How many sermons have we heard that are basically telling us that the darkness is an indicator that the end is imminent and we should be ready to evacuate Planet Earth at any moment? It's basically a call for the last one left to turn the lights off. God is obviously closing up shop soon. There is no denying the darkness that is prevalent in our world. We see the gross darkness show its insidious head in all kinds of things such as depression and anxiety dominating a generation of people. Wickedness and injustice occur on a scale perhaps never seen as it is on Planet Earth. The complexity of problems facing us justifiably causes many to give up hope in humanity's ability to turn things around.

But what if the darkness is not a countdown clock to the end of the world but a countdown clock to the dawning of a new day? What if God sees the darkness as the beginning instead of the end? The Bible seems to indicate that this is heaven's perspective.

> In the beginning, God created the heavens and the earth. The earth was without form and void, and darkness was over the face of the deep. And the Spirit of God was hovering over the face of the waters. And God said, "Let there be light," and there was light. And God saw that the light was good. And God separated the light from the darkness. God called the light Day, and the darkness he called Night. And there was evening and there was morning, the first day.
>
> —GENESIS 1:1–5

In the beginning, the very beginning, it seems that the darkness became the precursor to something God called "day." In fact, God called the light to emerge out of the backdrop of the darkness that was smothering this new world. The darkness wasn't the end of God's story of creation; it was the beginning point. God said, "Let there be light," and the world that was previously empty and void was filled with God's beautiful creation.

So from God's point of view, darkness is not a force that is encroaching upon His purposes or intentions; it merely is a void ready to be filled and chased away as soon as light first flickers.

Think about the church for a moment. Think about your own life and your testimony of what God has done in you. Think about where He found you when He revealed Himself to you and saved you. Everyone's story looks different, but in all cases, we were under the influence and the grip of darkness and death. Our lives were empty and chaotic, void of meaning and life. What we may have thought as the last word on our future became the starting point for God to flood us with new life, forming us into His beautiful new creation. Peter says it like this:

> But you are a chosen race, a royal priesthood, a holy nation, a people for his own possession, that you may proclaim the excellencies of him who called you out of darkness into his marvelous light.
>
> —1 PETER 2:9

His light that is now shining in the world is an announcement that in the midst of a world gone wrong, a world in which fear grips the hearts of humanity, God is very much at work. He has a light, a witness of His goodness and wisdom that is shining bright. The beginning of this new day, this new creation is His church. The church was not sent into the world to serve as a hospice for a world waiting for its time to run out. Absolutely not! We have been called out and sent back in as the carriers of God's light, God's truth, working in advance of the day that is already dawning.

> The night is far gone; the day is at hand. So then let us cast off the works of darkness and put on the armor of light.
>
> —Romans 13:12

Escapism as Our Response

This misconception is important to dismantle because the affect upon the church and its mission is incalculable. If the people God has placed in the world to be the light become overwhelmed by all of the wickedness and evil surrounding us, we may become tempted to buy into the pit of escapism. Escapism is fatalism dressed up in a spiritual costume. It is an attitude that takes its focus off of mission and purpose and begins to dream about getting out of here. Unfortunately the unprofitable response has become epidemic in some streams of evangelicalism. Often hidden within exaggerated end-time emphasis and teaching, Christians spend an inordinate amount of their time studying the different nuances of the Book of Revelation's exit plan and forget about the reason they are in the world in the first place. As long as we look at the darkness as an indicator that history has moved beyond the point of no return, we will never attempt to dispel it or address it.

When I was a senior in high school, the buzz around the Christian subculture was the release of a book that claimed to know the exact timing of the second coming of Jesus. It just so happened that the date the author predicted, based upon a complex system of Jewish feasts and numerology, would supposedly take place within a year of this book's anxious release. Needless to say, this book was selling off of bookshelves at the local Christian retail store quicker than it could be stocked. It created no small stir when the author claimed he was able to predict the time of this secret rapture of the church, encouraging people to prepare themselves.

I remember this because at that time I was a young Christian, fascinated with eschatology. I watched as well-meaning people got into heated arguments over the subject. Some people left churches altogether to await the *parousia* at home. Some ran up huge credit card bills assuming they wouldn't be here when the bills came due. Others even got witty bumper stickers stating that "This vehicle will be unmanned in case of Rapture" and the date printed boldly and in the face of the uninformed public.

I also remember how disappointed people were when the date that had been predicted came and went. The author went back to the drawing board to figure out where he had gone wrong and quickly published a revised version. It too failed, as did many people's faith. Their hopes of escaping this world had come and gone, and now they were left here to figure out what to do with their lives.

A little over a decade later the world was approaching the dawn of the new millennium, and there was a major focus centered around the upcoming power outage and potential system collapse that would almost certainly happen when the clock clicked over midnight on January 1, 2000. The crisis was shortened to the initials Y2K. People responded with paranoia and fear, stockpiling food and water, pre-paring for the end of the world as we knew it. Generators were selling off the shelves at outrageous prices to ensure survival when the lights went out. People went to great extremes believing that this modern world that had taken millennia to develop was about to collapse in a moment because of a programming mistake that couldn't be repaired in time. I even witnessed one family in my young church wheel-barrel soil down into their basements and begin to plant potatoes!

What concerned me the most was how the general church once again fell prey to all of the panic and propaganda. Many churches hosted conferences to "inform" people on the imminent doomsday scenarios. Ministries emerged that combined eschatology teaching with practical advice on how to protect your families. God-loving, Bible-believing, Spirit-filled Christians were buying guns and ammunition and making volatile statements about how they would shoot anyone who attempted to take their food or steal their property. I remember thinking to myself, "Is this how Christians should be acting? What about the Sermon on the Mount?"

Of course Y2K came and went, and no power outages were realized. Local pantries became the recipients of mass amounts of dried food and canned goods, and once again the church had been distracted by the darkness.

I find it ironic that in the process of preparing for the worst-case scenario, many people by their escapist mentalities allowed their own light to go out. While we spend the bulk of our time preparing to escape or defend our own security, we may be losing the opportunities that come our way to make a difference in someone else's life. If we don't see any future, we will never invest our time, talent, or resources in the present. This obsessive cycle of predicting the end of the world only to see it come to nothing has happened all throughout church history, and it always leaves the body of Christ damaged and demoralized. Unfortunately many of the institutions and avenues we so often curse and ridicule as the darkest of the dark are that way because in prior generations Christians were either too preoccupied with escapism or indifferent to the opportunity. Whenever there is a void or a vacuum within society left by a negligent church, hell is more than happy to take up residence.

The Bible is clear that Jesus will return to the earth one day, triumphantly to reign and rule over all. It should also be obvious that it was never God's intention for us to know the day or the hour—this is not our mission or purpose. While we eagerly look forward to the appearing of Jesus, our blessed hope, we should be energized and motivated to bring the gospel of Jesus Christ and the demonstration of His power to every shadowing place and corner of the globe that has not been previously penetrated. We aren't called to evacuate; we were called to occupy in anticipation of His return to reclaim the world that is rightfully His.

LIE #4: DARKNESS GROWS

What if I were to ask you, "What is the speed of light?" Would you know the answer? Maybe you would be able to remember back to your physics class and eagerly blurt out, "186,000 miles per second!", and you would be right. That means that the moment God spoke and said, "Let there be light," instantly the first rays of light speedily wrapped around the surface of the earth seven times in the first second of recorded history.

Let me ask you a trick question. "What is the speed of darkness?" Do you know the answer? Basically the answer is this: darkness doesn't technically have a speed because it is not a force. It is a void. Darkness *proceeds* at the exact speed that light *recedes*. I told you this was a trick question. Think about that statement for a moment. Darkness cannot independently move, shift, or create on its own. It can only occupy space at the speed that light pulls back or has not yet reached. As light grows stronger, it reaches farther.

The point of this little exercise is to help us understand that the darkness we witness in the world at large is not growing; it is instead hiding. The greatest threat to darkness is light becoming strong enough and confident enough that it reaches where the darkness reigns and destroys it. Darkness may cover, but darkness always exists on borrowed time. The devil may use the darkness of ignorance to blind the eyes of the lost, but as quickly as a spark of light can be struck, darkness must flee.

Years ago our church planned a father and son campout at a local state park. I am not much of a camper, so I was at a disadvantage when it came to having all the correct gear for our outing. I made a trip to the local outfitter and bought a tent, a couple sleeping bags, and a few of the necessities I thought we would need. My son, Jared, was about six at the time and was very excited to go on this adventure, so we left home earlier than we had planned and got there before anyone else. We spent some time setting up our tent, laying out our sleeping bags, and spraying on our bug spray just in time to see all our friends arrive.

We had strategically put our tent the farthest away we could from the parking lot so that we would not be disturbed all night by headlights and closing car doors. When dinner and the campfire stories were all done and it was time to turn in for the night, Jared and I made our way to the tent. The farther we got away from the others, the darker it got and the more difficult it was to see our way, and I had forgotten our new flashlight inside the tent. By the time we found our tent, we were completely blinded and resorted to groping around trying to feel our way in and find our flashlight so we could actually see something.

My new Maglite flashlight was a combination of a baseball bat and a utility light. I couldn't wait to see what it could do. The package it came in listed all the specs including the number of lumens of brightness it was capable of, but none of that meant anything to me. That is until I loaded the D batteries down the long tube, took it outside, and clicked it on. To my surprise the beam of light that came out of this light saber shot up into the air what seemed to be hundreds of feet. I twisted the bezel around the lens and watched as the light spread out into a broad swath that illuminated the entire area we were tripping through completely blinded a few moments before. It was amazing to see the power that came from this piece of metal.

This is a picture of the potential of every Christian. We can read the Bible and see all of the promises God gives us of supernatural power attached to our commission to go into all the world. We can read the stories of biblical heroes who did the impossible and overcame impossible odds. But to many of us those promises have no context because we just can't put those promises into context, just as all of the specs on the back of the package of the flashlight meant very little to me. The actual words made sense, but their message didn't translate until I actually put the batteries in and let it do what it was capable of.

The Bible will come alive in us when we actually put it into practice. The light that is in us won't shine brighter than when it is put on display in the darkest of circumstances and places. The church has no idea how powerful a force we can be as the light of the world. We have seen ourselves as the little keychain flashlight instead of the ever-increasing super nova moving across the face of the deep and exposing the world to the goodness and the beauty of our glorious God of grace. We have become so captivated by the thick darkness and its looming presence that we encounter every-where we look that our all too familiar human limitations keep us from doing anything about it. But the light of God's Word is more powerful than the deepest darkness. The light in you is greater than the darkness around you.

It's not until we actually become activated in our true

identity and understand the full scope of God's purpose for each of us that we will ever see the full brightness and potential of the glory of God working through us. Wherever we find darkness lurking, seemingly growing darker by the minute, that is the place to invade. This is not the time in history for us to pull up, pull back, or pull out. This is the hour for the church to arise. This is the time to fill your lamp with oil of passion for Jesus and His glorious cause and rush headlong into the fray. When the body of Christ becomes filled with the light of revelation and comprehends what the light is in each of us—hell will shake and darkness will flee, at the speed of light!

> The entrance of Your words gives light; it gives understanding to the simple.
>
> —PSALM 119:130, NKJV

Chapter 3

THE POWER OF ONE LIGHT

All the darkness in the world cannot extinguish the
light of a single candle.

—ST. FRANCIS OF ASSISI

D
AREN WAS LIVING the dream. Having graduated
from a storied Christian college, he found himself now fully immersed in the frenzied and often
unpredictable life of being a youth pastor in a growing
church. This was an obvious next step for him since his
degree fit well into this type of ministry, and he was still
relatively young and could relate to young people and the
challenges they face. Developing rapport and a ministry
focus that was committed to make a difference in the world
was no easy challenge, but Daren liked challenges.

During the summer of 2006 Daren took some time off
and set out on an adventure that he had been planning
for several months. Riding his bike across America from
Oregon to Virginia rekindled his passion for endurance
challenges, and soon he discovered that he felt more alive
out on the open road than in his church office. He loved the
thrill of not having a day planner to dictate when and where
he had to be at a certain time. Although he was missing out
on "normal life" as he had known it, he had also discovered that he enjoyed the physical discipline and all of the
unknown that waited for him down the road.

Along his journey he began to dream about what it would
look like if he were able to do this all the time. He loved
the Lord and enjoyed his job in youth ministry but had to

admit to himself that the thought of returning to his desk job made him feel spiritually claustrophobic. Long miles and hours to himself gave him time to think and pray about this dream that was stirring in his heart. If he could find a way to combine his dedication to serving others in the name of Jesus and his passion for adventure, he would sell all he had and leave everything behind. And that's exactly what he did when he got home.

After several months of planning and praying, Daren established a plan that would raise awareness and money to address the issue of clean drinking water in Africa. He had read the stories and seen the pictures of impoverished children dying of diseases that were avoidable with the implementation of clean wells and education. He decided he was going to do something about this problem and so began what became known as the Earth Expedition.

His goal was simple: walk around the entire earth to raise money and awareness to this global crisis that was affecting the poor and forgotten.

For his part he began walking what would ultimately become a 3,400-mile hike up the Appalachian Trail, taking six months to accomplish. Others signed up along the way to join in this mission by taking legs of the Earth Expedition in different continents. What started as a daydream and an inspired wish while riding his bike was now becoming a global movement.

A few years later as the vision expanded, Daren relocated to Kalamazoo, Michigan, to join up with his new partner who had helped refine the vision and the process into what became known as ActiveWater. Their goal: "to be an inspiration to people of all race, sex, gender, religion, and age and assist them in the unlocking of God-size dreams that will inherently change the world for another."[1] A ministry was born that partners with individuals and churches to turn whatever their passion is and whatever they can do to raise money and awareness to answer the problem of clean water globally in the name of Jesus. Last year Daren took this vision to a whole new level. He had decided a year earlier that he needed a new challenge, one that would also raise the stakes and shine a brighter light on the problem as well as the solution. The idea came to him, "What if I trained to swim across Lake Michigan to raise money to dig wells in Zambia?" He had never really swum seriously or any great distance, so this was well outside of his comfort zone, but he began to train anyway.

After hundreds of grueling hours in the pool and at the desk preparing for this momentous challenge, the day arrived. Daren took off out of New Buffalo, Michigan, for Chicago's Navy Pier. Supported by a team of volunteers on a guide boat and a few friends from Radiant Church kayaking next to him, the swim became more than he had bargained for. Having been moved off course by several miles because of the current and slowed by the choppy waves, Daren's swim went from the planned forty miles to over fifty (more than twice the distance of the English Channel swim) and took several more hours than had been planned. Exhausted and delirious, he made it to Chicago after thirty-five continuous hours of swimming without touching the bottom or placing a hand on a boat.

He ultimately had to be carried out of the water. His body was chaffed to the point of permanent scarring, and his pulse dropped dangerously low, below forty beats per minute. The medics immediately rushed him to the hospital, but not before Daren had completed his goal. He had not relented.[2]

Later Daren's heroic exploits spread as wildfire throughout the local media in the third largest city in the country. Phone calls came from every direction—from television and newspapers wanting to interview this crazy man who dared swim across the mighty Lake Michigan. He not only swam across the lake, but also he did it in a way no other had dared; he swam against the current!

During the next couple days Daren was interviewed by several local Chicago media outlets and was able to share the story of ActiveWater and his passion to serve other people in the name of Christ. His historic swim had now raised many thousands of dollars for clean water initiatives in Zambia and throughout Africa. Thousands of people living in some of the most remote places on the face of the earth that had never even heard of Lake Michigan would soon be given a gift that would impact them and their families for decades to come. They would have clean water in the name of Jesus and the true living water of the gospel— all because of one man's obedient response to swim against the current of darkness in this present age and dare believe that one light can make a difference. Daren is the epitome of what it means to be radiant.

SHADOWS OF DOUBT

Can one person's life really make a difference? I believe that most of us really struggle believing that the answer to this question is yes, especially when it comes to our one life. The world is so messed up and filled with so many complex and overwhelming problems. It's just too overwhelming to us to think we could do anything to change it. It seems as daunting to us as attempting to empty the Pacific Ocean with a bucket and shovel.

Every once in a while we see someone who does something that makes a significant difference or someone who is willing to get their hands dirtier than the rest, and we admire them greatly. Maybe we even think to ourselves, "I wish I could do something like that!" But that momentary spark of childlike faith evaporates, and we go back to living our lives of survival and surety. The breakdown comes because we can't quite figure out how God could possibly use someone as unqualified as us with our busy lives, unrelenting financial pressures, and hectic schedules.

The unfortunate thing about giving up the hope that we can actually do something to change the world around us is that somewhere in the process we end up losing ourselves. The truth is that each of us can and does affect the temperature of life around us. The people we know, the job we do, the team we coach, and the kids we raise—each of these is an avenue of influence where God has placed us. For good or bad we leave our mark all over these places and people, and the motive and vision that we bring with us day to day either illuminate or eliminate the presence of God with us.

Part of the problem is we underestimate what we are capable of doing right where we live, and we daydream to discouragement about where we wish we could go. We think the only way to truly turn the tide or impact people is "someplace else" and on a massive scale. While we all can't swim across Lake Michigan and earn thousands of dollars to change a continent, we all can swim against the current of apathy and shine brightly right where we live today. All of us can be encouragers, witnesses, servants, standard bearers, and givers. Any one of us is a candidate to *be* a miraculous answer to someone else's prayer.

The Bible tells us how Satan operates as a thief in our lives. Jesus said, "The thief comes only to steal and kill and destroy" (John 10:10). The way he carries out his thievery is subtle. The enemy of our souls doesn't show up at our doorstep and introduce himself, announcing his plans and strategies. He comes hidden in discouragement, condemnation, and distractions that ultimately rob us of a supernatural sense of purpose, killing any motivation or dreams we may have, and ultimately destroy the foundations that would hold up a life of servanthood that leads others to discover life and meaning in Jesus. This is diabolical, and it happens daily to countless saints.

I really believe so many Christians are bored and spiritually dying long before their time because down deep they sense, and even know, they were created to do something besides surviving, fitting in, and getting along. We know that we were meant to shake things up, turn this messed-up world right side up. We were meant to make a difference. But do we have it in us? Do we have what it takes? I believe the answer is unequivocally yes. Beyond a shadow of a doubt!

> For we are his workmanship created in Christ Jesus for good works, which God prepared beforehand, that we should walk in them.
> —EPHESIANS 2:10

IDENTITY CRISIS

Much of the problem facing the effectiveness of the church in the twenty-first century is not the devil, the pervasiveness of evil, or the culture war raging in the media. It is our own struggle to discover and own who we are, to see ourselves as God sees us, and to live out the intentions that Jesus had for us when He saved us and formed us as His body. We are suffering from a severe case of identity crisis. Until we come to an understanding of who we are in the world and why we are here, we will be more motivated out of insecurity than invincibility and allow the world to define us by their preferences instead of God's presence. It has been said that we will either be a prophet to our culture or a product of it. The choice is ours.

Too much time and too many resources have been spent over the last few decades trying to build a better "church trap." We have assumed the identity of convention centers, social clubs, talk shows, concert halls, revival meetings, social justice movements, and teaching institutions. All of these are fine and may indeed be descriptions of the activities that the church should be about, but they are not in and of themselves "who we are."

In our pursuit of fitting in and being accepted, the church has recalculated its theology to not offend, become more performance-driven, and scaled back evangelism to things that are not so overtly Jesus centered—all in the hopes that we will either draw crowds more effectively or be invited to have a place at the table of influence within our communities. But as soon as we compromise any of these things, we lose the power of these things. We have adopted words and concepts such as "relevant" and "seeker sensitive," both of which have their place, but we lose something of the power found in the message of the cross whenever we try to cut it and tame it. As C. S. Lewis described Aslan the lion, who symbolized Jesus in his classic book *The Lion, the Witch and the Wardrobe*:

> You mustn't press him. He's wild, you know. Not like a tame lion.[3]

Perhaps it is time for the pendulum to swing back toward embracing, unapologetically, the uniqueness and even peculiarity of the King whom we worship and the kingdom that we are a part of. As long as we are looking to the world to give us the nod of affirmation, we will be unable to shine as brightly as we should.

As leaders and pastors in the church, we too have done the people of God a disservice by creating an overemphasis on "coming to church" and not enough vision casting of what it means to "be the church." Gathering together to worship corporately is vital to our lives as believers, but it's inadequate if that's all we live for Monday through Saturday. Intentionally or unintentionally we have developed great crowds but unprepared people. The majority of the people who attend our churches do not know how to share their faith beyond just inviting people to church. Ministry is most often viewed as something that goes on "at the church" instead of "by the church." If our concept of ministry is restricted to our buildings, then we fall into the trap Jesus warned us against.

> Nor do people light a lamp and put it under a basket [insert "building" here], but on a stand, and it gives light to all the house.
>
> —MATTHEW 5:15

If ministry is viewed only as the expertise of hired clergy, that will not only sideline the majority of Christians on the bench of boredom but also limit the effectiveness of the mission of the church.

What would happen if a surge of energy and passion was infused into the heart and soul of the church in our day? Imagine what it would look like to see millions of believers who previously were unconvinced of their ability to make a difference with their lives, now fully alive, fully engaged in intentional ministry lifestyles, each of them operating from an understanding and confidence of God in them and at work through them. What will it take to get there? A new, or perhaps restored, picture of ourselves, painted by the Master Himself.

You Are...

Jesus did not have any doubt who we were meant to be. He wasted no time and minced no words in describing who you and I are.

> *You are* the salt of the earth; but if the salt loses its flavor, how shall it be seasoned? It is then good for nothing but to be thrown out and trampled underfoot by men. *You are* the light of the world. A city that is set on a hill cannot be hidden. Nor do they light a lamp and put it under a basket, but on a lampstand, and it gives light to all who are in the house. Let your light so shine before men, that they may see your good works and glorify your Father in heaven.
>
> —Matthew 5:13–16, nkjv, emphasis added

One day Jesus sat down on a hill beside the Sea of Galilee and taught the masses who had come out to hear Him. Jesus was unlike any other rabbi whom they had ever heard before. He taught with such conviction and authority but yet was compassionate and caring, as if He knew each of them. In reality He did know them, because He was one of them. He had grown up in this area and knew them and the typical lives that they were living. Now that He had begun His messianic announcement of the kingdom's presence, He didn't take off for the big city of Jerusalem where all the scholars, theologians, and movers and shakers were. He was traveling around Galilee bringing the good news of the kingdom of God to the small towns and villages of "everyday" people.

As Jesus sat down and began to teach what would become His *magnus opus* discourse, He was powerfully unveiling God's true intentions for His people and painting a picture of the identity of the children of God. He said to them:

"You are the light of the world," a "city set on a hill," and a "lit lamp on a stand."

As Jesus began to develop this metaphor, the people listening to Him must have had a strong sense of what He was referring to. There were many cities that may have come to mind that could easily be referred to in such a way.

Jerusalem was the spiritual capital of Israel, a city of such prestige and importance. This was where God had taken up physical residency on the earth, marking Israel as His people and Jerusalem as the city of the great King. Looking back, we see that Isaiah prophesied about the nations being drawn to the brightness of her rising. This was a prophetic "cause and affect" promise given to Israel foretelling of their restoration from exile and calling them back to their purpose to draw the nations back to God. When they were finally restored from exile and their hearts were fully alive to their destiny and purpose, they would once again be God's light to the nations of the world.

Every good Law-observing Jew understood the importance of Jerusalem to their relationship with God. Several times through their lives they would make a pilgrimage to this shining city. But Israel had rejected God and their place on the lamp stand of the nations. They had been restored to their land but missed their day of visitation for the most part.

Rome, the eternal city, was referred to as the light of the world.[4] The imperial city that governed most of the known world was a city set on seven hills, not just one. It was believed by every Roman emperor that it was their destiny to run the world and bless the nations they had conquered with civility and culture. This message of *Pax Romano* was the light that was now shining bright and the *gospel* that was spreading quickly. Rome was the largest and most powerful seat of political, military, and economic influence in the world at that time. The decisions made in these two cities on the hills impacted their lives in an almost complete fashion.

CITY ON THE HILL

Interestingly though, as Jesus teaches, He wasn't thinking of either of those two cities. The in-breaking of the kingdom of God had eclipsed the importance of both of those two cities and their power. He was announcing a shift that was to take place. The hope of the world was no longer (and never was) found in the governments of men or limited to a geographical center of spiritual elitism. The power and presence of God's increasing government was housed in earthen vessels and ordinary people, dispersed and positioned in unlikely places. This is the good news.

The most likely explanation of what Jesus was using as His illustration was the city of Sephoris.[5] Sephoris was a city that Jesus would've been well acquainted with. It is believed that Jesus's father, Joseph, moved the family to Galilee to work on the construction of this influential city. Jesus, learning the trade of carpentry at Joseph's side, would have walked the streets every day, as many of the other tradesmen of the area routinely did, and understood the importance of this place. Sephoris was built to be the seat of Herod Antipas's government in Galilee and was called the "ornament of all Galilee."[6] Jesus probably had this city in mind as He was now building His own "city on the hill" to be the beachhead of His ever increasing government upon the earth— His church.

Situated several miles from the Sea of Galilee and only three miles from Nazareth, it was visible from most villages that His listeners would have come from. Especially at night, when the darkness covered the huge lake and the hillsides, this "city on a hill" would illuminate the night. For the weary traveler a city such as this served as a bearing point to follow and offered hope of rest and protection from the harassment of bandits and robbers. It would have been very easy for Jesus to point to this elevated city and have them understand what He was saying.

The idea of being the light of the world was an overwhelmingly big picture. But the idea of a city set on a hill brought it closer to home because it was well within their line of sight and experience. This city was, in many ways, similar to every other neighborhood or community. It was not a beacon to the surrounding region because it had a single source of intense light. It's power and brilliance came as a result of thousands of lamps, set in thousands of windows in thousands of homes and buildings, collectively creating a single lit city that could not be ignored.

In the same way the significance of a single life cannot be underestimated. Jesus equates each of our lives as a lamp that is placed in a specific location with a specific purpose. Each person is a lamp set on a lamp stand, designed to give light to a single household. In the process of giving light in our specific places, we are also united together with the brilliance of thousands of other lamps, becoming a beautiful city that is giving light to the world.

LAMPS AND LAMP STANDS

One of the earliest symbols that Jesus used to describe His vision for each of us joined together as the church is a lamp on a lamp stand. Christians have used many different symbols throughout the ages to indicate different aspects of our faith—the fish or *icthus*, a shepherd and sheep, and of course the cross. While all of them are important and beautiful in their own way, the earliest of them all is that of a luminous lamp. The menorah, adapted from the temple motif, became a powerful description of the character and mission that Jesus had in mind for His followers.

It's not only in the Gospels that we see Jesus using this imaging, many years later when appearing to John the apostle on the island of Patmos during his exile, Jesus again identified the church and its role as lit lamps positioned on lamp stands of influence and assignment.

> The mystery of the seven stars which you saw in My right hand, and the seven golden lampstands: the seven stars are the angels of the seven churches, and the seven lampstands which you saw are the seven churches.
>
> —REVELATION 1:20, NKJV

It's interesting that lamps set upon lamp stands were used by Jesus to describe both the form and the function of each church. The Greek word used in the New Testament for this word *lamp* is derived from the word *luchnos*.[7] It is a word that describes a small, first-century terra cotta oil lamp that was common in most Middle Eastern homes. Unfortunately some translations of the Bible have translated "lamp" as "candlestick," giving the wrong impression that it is describing something like our wax candles. Such candles were not in use during this time.

These simple clay lamps that Jesus is referring to contained olive oil as fuel and burned a wool wick that would burn for hours once it was saturated with the oil. These small lamps that could be carried from room to room in the palm of the hand and placed upon an elevated pedestal were as common as electric lamps and light switches are in our homes today.

This perfectly described the dynamic of the believer's role in the world and the power and influence that each life can have. We are all human, mere earthen vessels who have received in Christ the oil of the Holy Spirit. We are called to be filled with this oil and willingly lit on fire with passion for Jesus and His cause. Wherever God has placed us, we are called there to bring the light. Light is a benefit to those who are in darkness. Light brings hope and perspective and illustrates what was previously unclear and unseen. That's what our calling is. It's not about doing one massive or monumental thing; it's about consistency and clarity in everything. It's about reflecting the image of God's character through our lives and actions.

The greatest mistake we can make is to do nothing because we can only do very little. But even the little, done well enough, long enough will change any environment. If you need an example of how this works, look at the Colorado River's impact upon the Grand Canyon—a massive canyon, slowly eroded by an unrelenting, ever moving current. This is the work of the Holy Spirit through the church.

Some of us will have huge kingdom assignments. Some of us will play the role of unsung heroes whose labor is never recognized in this lifetime. Some of us will impact millions, and others of us will impact one. All of us can make a difference in the brightness of our generation because all the darkness in the world, regardless how dark and seemingly powerful, cannot overcome one life lit brightly for Jesus. This is the calling and mandate of every single Christian: to be light bearers who shine brightly wherever He has placed us and believe that "God, who said, 'Let light shine out of darkness,' has shone in our hearts to give the light of the knowledge of the glory of God in the face of Jesus Christ. But we have this treasure in jars of clay, to show that the surpassing power belongs to God and not to us" (2 Cor. 4:6–7).

TAKE YOUR STAND

Last year I began a new hobby. I have always been a runner to one degree or another, but over the years it's been a love/hate relationship. I just seem to get bored with it sometimes but have always returned to it because I hate how I feel when I don't have an exercise outlet. Turning forty was a milestone year, and so I decided to either buy a Harley Davidson to medicate the midlife crisis or take up a new hobby. With the encouragement of my wife (the voice of common sense in my life) I passed on the motorcycle. But I did get a bike—a mountain bike, that is.

I had this guy, Mike, who had been a part of Radiant Church for years, invite me to join him and a few friends on a Tuesday evening to go mountain biking. I grew up riding BMX bikes, but it had been years since I had taken a serious bike ride. I almost blew it off, looking for some excuse why I couldn't do it, but instead I agreed to go.

Tuesday evening came around, and I almost bailed on him. I had had a long day at the office and was physically and mentally drained. Just about the time I was about to push "call" on my cell phone to let him down easy, I heard the honk of his horn out in the driveway. There was no going back now. I jumped in the car with him, and we headed out to the great unknown.

The first time out on the trails was exhilarating—painful but exhilarating. I wiped out a few times but for the most part did pretty good for my first time. I began to join Mike and several others from church each Tuesday night for the weekly ride. After several times riding, I decided this was for me and purchased a bike of my own and all the gear that goes with it. I had found a new hobby.

What impressed me most about our time out at these different riding trails was the subculture of people we were getting to know. I really had been unfamiliar up to this point with this community of people who rode seriously. I was unaware of the fact that Kalamazoo was known for having some of the best riding in the Midwest as well as one of the largest mountain biking populations in the country.

Most of them were avid outdoors enthusiasts, and like most subcultures, most of them were unchurched.

One night after a great ride several miles from home Mike and I were just having a casual conversation when he made a statement that opened up a much more serious and important topic. "I really wish I knew what my ministry was. I mean, I serve at church, but I don't feel like that's enough. I can't see myself teaching the Bible at this point or preaching or anything. I work with a bunch of people who don't have the same beliefs I do, and I only really feel 'Christian' on Sundays when we go to church, because that's when we are around our friends."

While he was talking, I was processing what I was hearing and thinking about how to respond to his question. I was kind of surprised by how he was discounting what God was doing through him. You see, Mike is one of those guys who gets along and connects with everyone. While I felt out of place around all of these mountain bikers and adventure racers, Mike knew them all. He had built great relationships with them. And you could tell that they all like him. He just had an uncanny ability to connect with these people because he loved the same sport they loved.

My response to Mike that night was, "Mike, do you understand that *this is* your ministry? Do you think it is any accident that God has placed you in the center of all of these people who are far from Christ and given you a platform? Most of them will never come looking for me because church is as foreign a concept for them as mountain biking has been for me. It took you to get me out here, and it'll take you to bring them to Jesus."

I could see in his eyes that the "lightbulb" went on inside of him. The reality and the practicality of God using us in ways we tend to overlook hit him. He was discovering that he was a lamp God had strategically put on a lamp stand within the mountain biking and adventure racing community. The relationships he had built were not just about bikes and orienteering; they were eternally intended to bring light to a house that others would never be invited to enter.

AN ARMY OF THE WILLING

What about you? Have you grasped the idea that God has placed you on a stand in a strategic place to give light to the people in that sphere of influence? If we could begin to see ourselves as a lamp in the order that Jesus described, then it would follow that we could also begin to intentionally and confidently live so brightly that others would see the goodness of God. Every house has a stand where the lamp is meant to be placed, and every household is unique to a specific family. What is the family that God has placed you in? Is it the school that you go to, the friends you hang with at the local coffee shop or work out with at the gym? Is it centered around your career or station in life? Is it your interest in art or a common struggle or loss that allows you to relate to others in a way that few others can?

I propose that the secret to our success in the kingdom comes down to seeing ourselves rightly and becoming increasingly aware of the place and time in which God has positioned us. Wherever you are, today is your lamp stand. Overlooking the significance and importance of where God has placed us is the equivalent to hiding our light under a basket of ignorance and underestimation. Allowing our inability to see ourselves as candidates to be used by God can keep us from taking our place on the high pedestal that can dispel the darkness and give light to everyone who is in that room. You are the light of your world—shine!

One person's candle is a light for many.

—THE TALMUD

The Bible is full of stories of one person's partnership with God that turns impossible situations around. None of them were qualified in the eyes of themselves or the skeptics. All of them had flaws and reasons why they couldn't or shouldn't.

One wanderer

Abraham was willing to leave everything familiar to him to follow the call of God to be a "father of a multitude" and to be a "blessing to all the families of the earth" who had no children and no road map of what lay ahead.

> By faith Abraham obeyed when he was called to go out to a place that he was to receive as an inheritance. And he went out, not knowing where he was going.... For he was looking forward to the city that has foundations, whose designer and builder is God.
>
> —HEBREWS 11:8–10

One dreamer

Joseph kept his dream alive even when it looked threatened and dead. He served with excellence and maintained his integrity in the pit of betrayal, with Potiphar's wife and household, in the prison, where he chose to serve others, and finally in Pharaoh's palace. His one idea and willingness to believe God and hold steady to the dream in the midst of overwhelming circumstances resulted in the saving of at least two nations and the very brothers who had betrayed him.

> As for you, you meant evil against me, but God meant it for good, to bring it about that many should be kept alive, as they are today.
>
> —GENESIS 50:20

One has-been

Think of Moses, who argued with God about all the reasons why he could not be the deliverer—a murderer, an exile wanted dead or alive, an ineloquent speaker, and a has-been with nothing left to give. But God challenged him with a question: "What do you have in your hand?" (See Exodus 4:2.) That stick became the rod of miracles that turned an empire upside down and parted a Red Sea. The power wasn't in the stick; it was in his willing obedience to the One who is more than all others combined.

One girl

Esther was a beauty queen winner, a newly crowned queen in the Persian Empire. When a law was passed to wipe out the entire Jewish race within Persia's borders, she was confronted with an opportunity to save her own life and let fear keep her quiet. What could one girl do in the face of such evil? Her cousin Mordecai's words prophetically called her to use her influence and favor to change the unchangeable. "Perhaps you have come into the kingdom for such a time as this?" were the words that drove her to turn the heart of the king and expose the diabolic motive of Haman and in the process save her nation.

> Then *I will go* to the king, though it is against the law, and if I perish, I perish.
> —ESTHER 4:16, EMPHASIS ADDED

Lest we think that this is only an Old Testament phenomenon, take a look in the second half of your Bible, and you will see the same affect of a single life willing to say yes.

One boy

A young boy passing by a great crowd listening to Jesus teach willingly volunteers his lunch to meet the need of thousands. Just a few loaves of bread and a couple of modest fish will never satisfy the hunger of thousands, but a single heart willingly surrendered to the miraculous multiplier feeds them all and leaves twelve baskets of leftovers for the doubting, cynical disciples to remind them that it's not about fish; it's about faith. His single, significant act ends up being the only other miracle recorded in all four Gospels beside the resurrection itself!

> There is a boy here who has five barley loaves and two fish, but what are they for so many?
>
> —JOHN 6:9

One widow

A widow who offers up her last mite in the offering box in the temple catches Jesus's attention and makes the Gospel record for all to remember the power of one life lit with willingness. Jesus said she gave more than everyone else because she gave out of her lack. She had something the others before her didn't. Not only was she aware of her lack, but she was also more aware of God's ability to use whatever we willingly give to Him.

> Jesus looked up and saw the rich putting their gifts into the offering box, and he saw a poor widow put in two small copper coins. And he said, "Truly, I tell you, this poor widow has put in more than all of them. For they all contributed out of their abundance, but she out of her poverty put in all she had to live on."
>
> —LUKE 21:1–4

One encourager Barnabas's name meant "son of encouragement." He was a man whom the Bible describes as noteworthy among the apostles and very generous with his resources. When the news began to spread about the supposed conversion of Saul of Tarsus, most were skeptical and afraid. This man had wreaked havoc upon the church. Many had been arrested, imprisoned, and even martyred as a result of Saul's best efforts. Now he wanted to have fellowship with the very people he had spent his life and career hating. Most did not want to have anything to do with him for obvious reasons and doubted whether he was a true believer. Barnabas went and found this discouraged disciple and brought him to the apostles. His words of affirmation gave Paul an open door to the fellowship of the church and eventually to fulfill the call of God on his life to bring the gospel to the Gentiles in uncharted territories.

Whatever words Barnabas used to encourage Paul and open the door for him before the leaders of the church would eventually have a ripple affect. Paul the apostle would eventually write two-thirds of the New Testament and expand the horizons of the burgeoning church to those beyond Jews. How important were those words of one encourager? Imagine if there had not been an encourager in Paul's life.

LIGHT YOUR CANDLE

Now ask yourself a question: Whose encourager could you be? What miraculous turnaround is waiting on the other side of your faith-filled, willing response to God's ridiculous invitation? Where is the lamp stand you have been trying to get down off of but God wants you to shine from? Could it be that you have come into the kingdom for such a time as this? I believe the answer is yes. You were not meant to be hidden or disguised. You were meant to be out in the open and highly visible. You are a light, *the* light of the world.

As long as we remain discouraged or in doubt about the difference our lives can truly make, we will remain in the dark with our lives unlit. You were not created to be a showpiece; your design was made for function and form. Jesus called you a light and a lamp for a reason. That's who you are, and you were made to shine in the place where He has positioned you. Take a look at where you find yourself situated in life. If it seems dark, if it seems empty and void, the odds are you are there for a reason. Lamps were made for dark rooms. Not to blend in, but to shine and give light and definition to those who are blinded and groping for hope. The enemy wants to discourage you and keep you toned down. He would love nothing more than to snuff out the flame from your life. But you and I are the ones who make that call. God has filled us with the oil of His Holy Spirit and placed us where it pleases Him. We have to strike the match and grab the flame. We have to be aware and willing.

God is building an army of willing ones. One by one we are beginning to see ourselves as a part of something bigger than ourselves. We are carriers of a kingdom that is shining brighter and brighter day by day. The kingdom I am part of is so much bigger than the part I play alone. But the part I am called to play is invaluable to the overall picture of God's purpose being complete. I am one candle, burning on a lamp stand, in one house, in one window, but I am shining my part and joining in with the brilliance of countless others as a city set on a hill and a light to the world! We are but one light, but we are impossible to extinguish. Wherever we go, wherever He sends us, we are destined to dispense the life of God and banish the darkness.

> That you may be blameless and innocent, children of God without blemish in the midst of a crooked and twisted generation, among whom you shine as lights in the world.
>
> —Philippians 2:15

Chapter 4

COLOR YOUR WORLD

I will be color to the black and gray, I'll raise a banner up in Jesus' name, I will be love lit on fire, Holy Spirit, burn on the inside.[1]

—JARED ANDERSON

Here's another way to put it: You're here to be light, bringing out the God-colors in the world. God is not a secret to be kept. We're going public with this, as public as a city on a hill. If I make you light-bearers, you don't think I'm going to hide you under a bucket, do you? I'm putting you on a light stand. Now that I've put you there on a hilltop, on a light stand—shine! Keep open house; be generous with your lives. By opening up to others, you'll prompt people to open up with God, this generous Father in heaven.

—MATTHEW 5:14–16, THE MESSAGE

L AST YEAR THE television in our bedroom conked out on us during a severe Michigan blizzard. There isn't much to do on days such as this other than watch TV and do your best to stay warm. My kids were pumped because school had been canceled and were all gathered in the favorite room in our house, Jane's and my bedroom. I grabbed my son, Jared, and together we headed out into the winter wonderland in my four-wheel drive. Destination? Walmart to buy a new television.

To be honest, I really wasn't too upset about the prospect of having to buy a new television. I had had my eye on one of the new thinner units with a super-clear picture.

For months every time that we went to Walmart, I made my pilgrimage to the back of the store to stare longingly at the latest and the greatest models. I knew it wouldn't be long before we would bring one of these beauties home with us, and today was that day!

We ended up with a 32-inch LED that was super thin and had a brilliant picture that almost seemed 3D. I could not wait to get it home, out of the box, and hooked up so we could spend all afternoon numbing our minds with Sports Center and random home improvement shows (as well as baby programs that the female majority in our home was sure to demand). With a little help from my son, we got it mounted on our wall, plugged it in, and hooked up to the cable box. We jumped on the bed with our whole family gathered, anticipating the moment when she would come to dazzling life. As the screen lit up, there was a moment when everyone "oohed" and "awed" at the brilliance of the high-def monitor. It was as if we were watching television for the first time. Needless to say, the new TV was a hit.

Now I wasn't alive when the first television show was broadcast and became a mainstay of American culture, but I can only imagine that it had to be a momentous occasion. I do, however, remember the first time I watched a color television. I was five years old, and my grandparents had just purchased a top-of-the-line cabinet color television for the front room. You know, the kind that could double as a coffee table and became the center of the living room, holding family pictures and retirement clocks. I remember my grandfather calling me into the family room. "Sit down on the floor," he said with excitement. "Watch this! You're not going to believe what you see!" As the screen began to warm up and the picture grew from a white speck on the screen to a larger picture eventually filling the whole curved glass tube, my eyes about popped out of my head. "This is incredible!"

I still remember the first program I ever watched on that color television. It was one of my favorite cartoons I had previously watched every day, but with the color television it was as if I was watching it for the first time all over again. It seemed to leap off the screen, and I could see the colors and textures in a way that seemed to make it look as if it were real life. It was sensory overload, and I couldn't get enough of it. Television watching would never be the same.

My good friend Mike Popenhagen, who has also been the worship leader alongside me for the whole journey of building Radiant Church, once told me about his first experience seeing a color TV. "The first time I saw a color television I remember thinking to myself, 'When did the world become color?' I really thought that 'television world' had only been black and white until something must have happened that turned the world to color. I thought the shows that were black and white truly reflected the way the world was and now that the same shows were in color, it must've been because someone turned the color on in the world. Apparently everything had changed."

I think in many ways Mike's conclusion was not far from the truth—not because the world somehow switched to color as a result of some new technological advancement, but the world indeed has had a moment when it went from black and white to full color. I believe there was a defining moment in history in which this world that had existed only in gray scale was introduced to a palette of brilliant, vibrant colors that changed everything—that moment was connected to a person. And that person was and is Jesus.

All that humanity knew about God had been limited to what was read in those bold black letters written upon the whitened parchments of the law, the Old Testament. But Jesus, the Word of God, came living, breathing, healing, and teaching in red letters like no one else had before Him, giving to the world for the first time, a high-definition, Technicolor version of what God was really like.

A WORLD GONE BLIND

The prophet Isaiah had it right when he described the world under the heavy blanket of darkness.

> Darkness shall cover the earth, and thick darkness the peoples.
>
> —ISAIAH 60:2

Darkness ruled over the hearts and lives of all humanity, manifesting itself in sin, violence, and distance from the divine. A world that originally was created in beauty and goodness had become lost under the shroud of blinding darkness. It seems when Adam's and Eve's eyes were opened as a result of their temptation and treason that in another way their eyes were also blinded to the way things were supposed to be.

> Then the eyes of both were opened, and they knew that they were naked.
>
> —GENESIS 3:7

They immediately saw that they were naked—stripped of their regal glory and eternal life. This became the way they saw everything else—naked and absent of the God-beauty that they had been given as a gift connected with God's purpose and presence. Now the world they were originally given authority over was bare and naked once again. The darkness, or absence of God's presence and glory, became a terminal blindness to them and would drive them from the land called Eden or "place of beauty" out into a world of dark uncertainty and loss. The vitality and color had been stripped from everything, and all that was left was a hollow, gray version of what once was and was always supposed to be.

For them the world under the influence of spiritual darkness may have been much like looking at an object from a distance that is sitting in front of a window. As the daytime passes and the sunlight fades, the object that just a few moments ago may have been vibrant and rich in color is now just a shape and a shade becoming less and less visible. It falls under the spell of darkness and loses all definition. In reality the object hasn't changed at all, but our ability to observe it in detail has become affected, and our eyes have failed to adjust because of the lack of light. We are the problem. We find ourselves seeing but not really seeing.

The world has become blinded and unable to see the world, ourselves, each other, or God the way that they were meant to be seen. We have become blinded to our own condition, groping through life trying to find our way, stumbling over ourselves, our ignorance, and one another.

This blindness brought on by the darkness of our sin, and rebellion is the favorite tool of Satan in his all-out effort to manipulate humanity's lost condition and keep it in bondage.

> And even if our gospel is veiled, it is veiled only to those who are perishing. In their case the god of this world has blinded the minds of the unbelievers, to keep them from seeing the light of the gospel of the glory of Christ, who is the image of God.
>
> —2 CORINTHIANS 4:3–4

The adversary is relentless in his work to keep us from ever regaining our sight. His all-out efforts to keep us deceived, distracted, and distanced from the truth is his only pursuit, and the result of it is a world that has no idea of what beauty and love really are. We are kept in the dark because of our guilt and shame and unable to live as we were meant to. We are under the deception of the enemy.

> So we are lying if we say we have fellowship with God but go on living in spiritual darkness; we are not practicing the truth.
>
> —1 JOHN 1:6, NLT

From the very beginning the devil has been a liar and a murderer. He came tempting Adam and Eve with the intentions all along of separation—separation from the life of God. His main objective was to get our eyes off of God and onto ourselves, knowing that such a decision would bring a fatal spiritual blindness and a progressive onset of death. The beauty of their relationship with the Creator and their destiny assignment to rule and reign over a world of beauty and vibrant testimony to the wisdom of God was now stripped from them, and the lights went out, leaving them in a world of shadows and gloom. Since then every generation has been born into a world that is just a shell of what it used to be, unaware that so much has been lost. Our eyes open the day we are born, but we are able to see only the aftermath and not things as they were originally created to be.

For each of us it is difficult to believe or embrace what we have never known—even if there is a sense that there must be something more, something real. Satan is a master manipulator and utilizes and distorts our view of everything that God originally made very good. Sex, the character of God Himself, true love, justice, success, and significance are all arenas that we have only seen the outline, as in a darkened room, but not the full detail and rich, full-color goodness.

Now we see things imperfectly, like puzzling reflections in a mirror, but then we will see everything with perfect clarity. All that I know is partial and incomplete, but then I will know everything completely, just as God now knows me completely.

—1 CORINTHIANS 13:12, NLT

In the absence of this detail our imaginations fill in the gaps, and that is a dangerous thing when our minds are continually wicked and twisted by sin's dark influence. This is where we need truth's light to come in. Light is the only thing that can bring truth and revelation to those things that have been hidden in darkness and distorted by falsehood.

God made it clear that in spite of mankind's rebellion and resulting penalty, He was not willing to leave the world lost in the darkness. There would come a day, a specific day, when God would send a light into the world that would restore the beauty and definition of His good intentions. Out of an area of obscurity, where no one would look for it, God would astonish the world and send His only Son into it as the Light of the world.

But there will be no gloom for her who was in anguish. In the former times he brought into contempt the land of Zebulun and the land of Naphtali, but in the latter time he has made glorious the way of the sea, the land beyond the Jordan, Galilee of the nations. The people who walked in darkness have seen a great light; those who dwelt in a land of deep darkness, on them has light shone.

—ISAIAH 9:1–2

SIGHT AND SOUND GOD

The apostle John was by all counts closer to Jesus than most. He describes himself as the disciple Jesus loved (John 13:23) and was one of the three who made up Jesus's inner circle of disciples. In the final moments of Jesus's suffering upon the cross, John was the one commissioned by Jesus to take care of His mother, an expression of love and deepest trust.

The Gospel that John wrote, as well as the Epistles that bear his name, reveal a perspective of the life of Jesus that is different than the other Gospel writers reveal. His are written from a closer, more intimate proximity than the others and describe the life of the Messiah in an attention-to-detail, up-close-and-personal viewpoint. John begins his first Epistle by describing what it was like to follow Jesus firsthand and up close. The impact on those called to walk with Him and behold Him in the flesh had radically rein-terpreted their view of God and life altogether. In John's view this mystery called the "incarnation" had now become the doorway for the sight of a world gone dark to finally be restored.

> That which was from the beginning, which we have heard, which we have seen with our eyes, which we have looked upon and have touched with our hands, concerning the word of life—the life was made mani-fest, and we have seen it, and testify to it and proclaim to you the eternal life, which was with the Father and was made manifest to us—that which we have seen and heard we proclaim also to you, so that you too may have fellowship with us; and indeed our fellowship is with the Father and with his Son Jesus Christ. And we are writing these things so that our joy may be complete.
>
> —1 JOHN 1:1–4

Being good Jewish boys growing up in Israel, attending synagogue, and hearing the Torah read every week, they would have developed a pretty good internal picture of who they thought God was and what He was like. That is the way the imagination works in all of us. We combine our perceptions, our learned knowledge, and our experiences together and craft an image of what we believe God must be like.

But when Jesus called each of His disciples to leave their old lives behind and to follow Him, they were able for the first time to "see" and "hear" and "touch" God firsthand. Part of the call to follow Him was also a call to leave that old paradigm behind and to discover the full beauty and reality of who the Great I Am really is. What they experienced many times was in contradiction to what they had been told God was like or what they had previously expected Him to be. Now they were walking with God in the flesh incarnate, Immanuel.

Can you imagine what that must have been like to look up in front of you and see "God" leading the way down the dusty path, to watch His attention shift to the obscure blind man on the side of the road and watch as compassion oozed out of Him, resulting in his sight being restored? How overwhelming it must have been to watch the righteous anger rise up within Jesus, the veins in His neck bulging as He turned over tables in the temple because the injustice and corruption were too much for Him to take. Every day was a never-ending process of realizing who God really was.

It seems from reading the Gospels that the disciples struggled at times in their attempt to figure out who this rabbi really was and where He fit into their theology. They didn't quite have a grasp on the doctrine of the incarnation and the implications or what His role was going to fill and how it would affect them and all of Israel, much less the world. They did believe He was Messiah, the Savior, and an anointed prophet.

The religious leaders were even more in the dark about Jesus. Their own religious bias and sense of entitlement blinded them from fully buying in and ultimately led them to seek out His death. Jesus did not fit into their box, so they rejected Him. But Jesus continued to make statements to them that revealed He was much more than a prophet or a political or spiritual leader. He was indeed God who had come in the flesh, in part to reveal who and how God is, who He has always been. Think about these statements Jesus made to them about Himself:

> "Your father Abraham rejoiced that he would see my day. He saw it and was glad." So the Jews said to him, "You are not fifty years old, and have you seen Abraham? Jesus said to them, "Truly, truly, I say to you, before Abraham was, I am."
>
> —JOHN 8:56–58

> My sheep hear my voice, and I know them, and they follow me. I give them eternal life, and they will never perish and no one will snatch them out of my hand. My Father, who has given them to me, is greater than all, and no one is able to snatch them out of the Father's hand. I and the Father are one.
>
> —JOHN 10:27–30

> Phillip said to him, "Lord, show us the Father, and it is enough for us." Jesus said to him, "Have I been with you so long, and you still do not know me, Philip? Whoever has seen me has seen the Father."
>
> —JOHN 14:8–9

Jesus was pulling back the veil of mystery and making it clear that He was much more than they had bargained. He was the expressed image of the Father.

> For in him all the fullness of God was pleased to dwell.
>
> —COLOSSIANS 1:19

"If you want to know what God was like, take a look at Me. Because I am." What a bold statement that is. For three and a half years they were able to see this "sight and sound" God who was no longer a theory or philosophical ideal. God had taken up a physical address, and Jesus was His name. Everything that Jesus did, every healing, every sermon, every moment of joy and sorrow, every tear He shed, and every prayer He prayed gave them a more vivid understanding of who God really was. Jesus was in every detail, every pixel, and every note, exactly as God truly is. Jesus is and was perfect theology.

Not only was this true for the disciples, but also it was true of everyone who encountered Jesus firsthand. For the first time we were able to fully comprehend the true nature and heart of God. The crowds were magnetically drawn to Jesus because there was something different about Him that they couldn't quite put their finger on. He was a man with uncommon compassion, supernatural power as no other, and the message of the kingdom of God that offered hope to the most hopeless and offered life, real life, to all.

Jesus met their needs, great and small, practical and spiritual, and was unafraid to touch the untouchable and notice the overlooked and forgotten. Jesus was busy, painting a picture throughout the villages and towns of Israel. Every healing was another masterful brushstroke. Every word spoken of the kingdom of God added another layer and brilliant color on the canvas of their perception. He was

the embodiment of all that the heart of God contained—
pure beauty. In Jesus, the Word made flesh, grace and truth
finally met.

GRACE AND TRUTH RESTORED

> And the Word became flesh and dwelt among us, and
> we have seen his glory, glory as of the only Son from
> the Father, *full of grace and truth*. (John bore wit-
> ness about him, and cried out, "This was he of whom
> I said, 'He who comes after me ranks before me,
> because he was before me.'") For from his fullness
> we have received, grace upon grace. For the law was
> given through Moses; *grace and truth* came through
> Jesus Christ. No one has ever seen God; the only God,
> who is at the Father's side, he has made him known.
>
> —JOHN 1:14–18, EMPHASIS ADDED

Jesus was the perfect expression of every aspect of God's
true nature. John chose a phrase to describe Jesus that clar-
ifies this balance and completeness: "grace and truth." In
contrast to the law given by Moses that became a yardstick
of unyielding and emotionless truth, the Word made flesh
put the life back into the truth revealed.

Isn't it interesting that when God originally revealed the
Law, it was not in written form but rather spoken, breathed
from the mouth of a God who was personal and present.
Moses had brought them to the foot of Mount Sinai and told
the people to prepare their hearts and consecrate themselves.
The God who had spoken to Moses out of a burning bush
descended in fire and clouds upon the top of the mountain
of the Lord and gave them His law. The people were undone
by the presence of the Lord. Their sinfulness and shame
were exposed in the unveiled revelation of a holy God, and
they were overwhelmed. Their solution? To send Moses up

to God and have him dictate what God required of them to live, but don't let Him speak to them any longer. What a tragic day in Israel's history. They wanted to exchange a person for a precept.

From that day forward the Law became a lifeless, two-dimensional taskmaster that mercilessly convicted every man and woman of their sin without hope or prejudice. Men in their pride began to interpret and define what the requirements of the Law were, and instead of it becoming a life-giving manifesto of a people in loving relationship with the heavenly Father, it became a constant reminder of how sinful and broken they were and how hopeless the pursuit of earned righteousness really was.

What was lost at the bottom of Mount Sinai was regained at the top of Mount Calvary. The God who loved the world and had committed Himself to redeeming humanity would not be put off for long. In spite of Israel's refusal to draw near to the presence of God hidden in the darkness of the cloud on top of Mount Sinai, this God would come down the mountain in pursuit of the ones He loved. Jesus came to restore the true image of God that had been marred once by Adam and marred again by a Law centered only in unwavering rules and requirements. He came not to detract from the truth of the Law but to complete it. The missing element was grace. In other words, Jesus came as the Word, the full expression of the truth, but yet His motive and intention were mercy and not judgment. This was the driving force in the ministry and teaching of Jesus.

He came into the world as the light of the world, shedding light and exposing everything wrong with this world but more importantly demonstrating everything that is right with God.

In him was life, and the life was the light of men. The light shines in the darkness, and the darkness has not overcome it....The true light, which gives light to everyone, was coming into the world. He was in the world, and the world was made through him, yet the world did not know him. He came to his own, and his own people did not receive him. But to all who did receive him, who believed in his name, he gave the right to become children of God, who were born not of blood nor of the will of the flesh nor the will of man, but of God.

—JOHN 1:4–13

The Incarnation, God coming in human flesh, is a great mystery. Great thinkers and theologians have spent two millennia attempting to wrap their minds around this truth and how such a miracle could take place. What is beyond dispute is the result. The world went from black and white to Technicolor in the fullness of time in which Jesus, the Savior, came into the world. What He left behind is a full-color, sight-and-sound masterpiece that culminated with the ultimate expression of the full spectrum of God's grace and love: the cross. To think that God would sacrifice Himself at the hands of His own creation for the salvation of a rebellious people who did not fully understand or recognize what God was up to is astounding to say the least. It was not force that kept Jesus upon that cross; it was sheer love. The darkness of hate and violence did not overwhelm Him. In His death He once and for all broke the power of sin and death. His red blood flowing down His open arms matched His red-letter words, reformatting the world and filling it with hope and life. In His death the light was not extinguished, only magnified, exposing the greatness of God. Three days later a new day dawned. As the first rays of light peaked over the horizon that first Easter morning, the stone had already been rolled away and the Son of God had risen. A new day, a new creation had dawned, and the love of God was about to sweep over the face of the earth at the speed of light.

This resurrection of Jesus would turn the world upside down and open the eyes of His followers, causing them to see God, reality, and the part they were now playing in the purpose of God from a whole different angle. The brush and the palette had now been handed off to His church, and He was now ready to paint this world with the brilliant colors of grace and truth. The church He had created and filled with His very Spirit is *now* the light of the world, commissioned to re-present God in full color to a world that had only known a distorted view of God. He commissioned them to take their place in the world and be salt and light, allowing the life of Christ to be on display in them and through them.

The Church: The Spectrum of Grace and Truth

When I was very young, it was obvious to my parents and teachers I had a very creative and artistic nature. I loved to draw, act out dramatically, and create things. I spent long hours by myself developing my abilities and noticing things many others just seemed to take for granted. One the things I was most fascinated by was this piece of glass my science teacher had proudly sitting on the end of his desk. I was captivated by it because of what happened at certain times of the day when the light would hit it just right. A rainbow of colors would shoot out the other side of it onto the wall when the light pierced its side. Sometimes this was intentional on the part of my teacher, and other times it just happened as the light came through the classroom window.

Whenever it did happened, my full attention shifted to this brilliant display and trying to figure out how it was happening. I tried it at home with a glass bottle, but to no avail. There was something special about this other piece of glass. My elementary school teacher was a very clever man to lure such inquisitive minds such as mine to pay attention in science class. When I finally asked about it, Mr. Prinns explained to me the principles of the prism. This wasn't just a piece of glass after all, but a specifically designed crystal that would slow down white light as it entered it and refract and reflect the light in such a way that the various colors of the spectrum were made distinct and visible. It made what was invisible visible.

I think there is a lesson the church can learn about itself in the physics of how a prism works. As the light passes through the prism, the colors are released. As God's light of grace and truth moves through the lives of His people, the full spectrum of the colors of God's beauty and goodness is revealed to a world that is otherwise color-blind and color deprived.

We become reflectors of the glory of God. This is the purpose of God for the church: to open the eyes and hearts of the world to a God who is other than what they may have thought, to put Jesus on full display, and to demonstrate the full grace and truth of God lived out through our flesh-and-blood lives in order to attract the attention of a veiled world.

> For God, who said, "Let light shine out of darkness,"
> has shone in our hearts to give the light of the knowl-
> edge of the glory of God in the face of Jesus Christ.
> —2 Corinthians 4:6

This was the model of Jesus. He was the walking embodiment of truth but the full expression of grace at the same time. This balance was in no way a compromise. Jesus was not a lesser expression of truth than the Law was. To the contrary, He was an even more precise bearer of the truth of God but not to the exclusion of grace. His extension of grace is the place where unwavering judgment and condemnation revealed the character and intentions of the Father.

Because grace and truth were the modus operandi of Jesus, it therefore becomes a good starting point for each of us to evaluate how God would potentially use us to impact others lives. If we desire to impact the world in the same way of Jesus, these two channels of light must be continually flowing through us as light through a prism, and we must be angled in such a way that we are giving off the complete spectrum of the God-colors to a black and gray world.

In his book *Beauty Will Save the World* Brian Zahnd sums this passing of the baton from Jesus, the incarnate Light of the world, to us, His church, in this way:

> We see the eternal and invisible God only in incarnation. Apart from incarnation, "no one has ever seen God." Of course the supreme incarnation of God is the Incarnation of Christ. But God continues his work in the world through incarnation in the lives of ordinary people who are willing to love and serve others in the name of Christ.[2]

We must recognize and cooperate with exactly how it is that God would use us, His church, to effectively reflect His glory to the world around us in very "flesh and blood" ways, embracing our role of helping other people see God in a way that is not normal but super-normal, filled with the same grace that rescued us. It's as if the picture of God, like those in a child's coloring book, has been drawn in the pages of Scripture, but then He uses us to be the coloring crayons that fill in the color to complete the revelation.

There are three specific ways I see in Scripture that the wisdom (or truth) and the grace (underserved favor and attention) of God are demonstrated through the church as light through a prism, coloring our world.

OUR STORY

I believe that one of the most powerful tools in the life of a Christian is their own personal story of redemption. How was it that you came into the light and personally experienced God's grace? Humans are designed to remember stories instead of bullet points. We were wired to tell stories and to be impacted by stories of others because stories connect us. They give rhyme and reason, purpose and meaning to our lives in a world that is formless and void.

There is not a more powerful story than God's story. That's really what the Bible is—a compilation sixty-six books full stories of ordinary people who intersected with an extraordinary God at the point of grace and truth. It is a large (or meta) narrative beginning with a God who loves, purposes, creates, reveals, redeems, and finally restores. It is the middle of God's story that we find our own. The stories of other men and women who encounter God become our point of faith and hope. Their stories become lessons for us as we try to make sense out of our stories. It's in these stories that we find the likes of Ruth and Rahab, Peter and Paul, and we see the full spectrum of God's ability and mercy.

Every Christian has a testimony about how God has saved, healed, or changed their lives whether or not we acknowledge it as significant. We seldom share what we underestimate, and unfortunately there is a correlation between the number of Christians who see their God story as less important or potent and the number of Christians who share their faith. The two are interconnected. Most people who receive Christ don't do so as a result of an altar call.

Long before the altar call they have heard from someone they trust or look to, and it's their miraculous story that opens the door for the black letter gospel message to take on "flesh and blood." It stirs the soul to believe that this is a God who cares and can also save them from their sins or heal them from the sickness or oppression.

When I was a teenager and fairly young in the Lord, I used to go to a prayer meeting on Wednesday evenings after youth group. The room would fill up quickly with about twenty to thirty other young people ready to testify and pray. Part of the time we spent preparing to pray was going around the room and giving people an opportunity to testify to something that God had done for them during the last week. Many times this became a moment for someone to share about how they had recently committed their life to Christ and how they had been delivered from a lifestyle of sin and shame. The people sitting in that circle would listen intently with eyes wide open as many made-for-television testimonies were given about being saved from lives of debauchery and wild sin. Everyone would give praise to God for delivering such a one out of the darkest of sin and bringing them into His kingdom.

To be honest, most of the time I felt more discouraged than encouraged, mostly because I really didn't feel that I had much of a story to share. I have to admit there were times I wished I had been saved from drug addiction or some other shocking background because as ridiculous as it is, my story didn't seem dramatic enough. I grew up in church for the most part. I had always had a love for God and prayed several times to make sure I was a Christian. I had never experimented with drugs or alcohol. My small temptations seemed insignificant in comparison to those I heard from others. My wish to have a more dramatic conversion testimony was not out of some feeling that I had missed out on those things, but because I thought that if I had a story "like that" all of my friends would accept Jesus and I could be used as a witness to God's amazing grace. As it was, I underestimated my story, but only because I overlooked the fact that every story is unique and God's grace can be found in every believer's story. We just have to have eyes to see it.

The Bible says:

> But God, being rich in mercy, because of the great love with which he loved us, even when we were dead in our trespasses, made us alive together with Christ—by grace you have been saved—and raised us up with him and seated us with him in the heavenly places in Christ Jesus, so that in the coming ages he might show the immeasurable riches of his grace in kindness toward us in Christ Jesus.
>
> —EPHESIANS 2:4–7

Each of us can find our story in this scripture. This is our story—all of us. We just have to look for the fingerprints of God's grace all over our lives that testify to God's loving grace that pursued and saved us. And as with every other great story, we have to tell it. Tell it far and wide and tell it with passion. There is something about a person's testimony that breaks through all the arguments. You can argue dogma or doctrine, but it is impossible to argue with someone's experience. When we tell others about a personal God who isn't just a questionable deity hidden in outer space, but rather a God who has supernaturally changed us and our story, the light begins to shine and hope arises in others.

Sometimes the only thing that can penetrate through the veil blinding an unbeliever is the power of a testimony. It's one thing to know the bullet points of what Christianity is all about or to be presented with the Four Spiritual Laws or the Roman's Road, but those same principles lived through a person's life bring out the colors of God's goodness. It takes on high definition and Technicolor reality when it is your life story that walked down that Roman's Road and can tell someone else what God graciously has done in your life.

> And they overcame him by the blood of the Lamb and by the word of their testimony, and they did not love their lives to the death.
>
> —REVELATION 12:11, NKJV

Your testimony of how God's grace and truth moved through your story and brought eternal life to you brings God's bigger story of salvation into the here and now in full color. Like weaving a tapestry, God has intricately stitched together a masterpiece in the way He cares and saves each of us. Our story brings the power of Jesus's victory on the cross into the present possibility of others. There is a chromosome of "overcoming" in the DNA of our relationship with God.

OUR GIFTS

> As each person has received a gift, minister it to one another, as good stewards of the manifold grace of God. If anyone speaks, let him speak as the oracles of God. If anyone ministers, let him do it as with the ability which God supplies, that in all things God may be glorified through Jesus Christ, to whom belong the glory and the dominion forever and ever, amen.
>
> —1 PETER 4:10–11, NKJV

One of the ways the full spectrum of God's grace is manifest is through the various gifts and abilities He places within the lives of His people. Each of us has been given specific grace-empowered gifts to serve one another and give witness to the brilliance of God. Jesus said that the aim of our good works and the point of our being placed in specific, strategic places are to shine—shine in such a way that God receives the glory and not us. When we let the world see the goodness of God through the things we do and the way that we do them, their eyes will be filled with the light of truth and see another side of God that may not have been visible to them before.

Peter tells us without any hesitation that we have each received a gift. None of us have slipped through the cracks. He paints a picture with the choice of his words, inspired by the Holy Spirit, that help us understand what it means to "color our world." He uses the word *manifold* to describe what grace in a believer's life looks like.

The word *manifold* is translated in some other translations as "varied," "variety" or "variegated." This word is translated from the original Greek word *poikilos* and can mean "many colored" or "multisided." This word has a similar meaning to what we describe as a prism. God has chosen to create each of us uniquely, with different angles in our spiritual DNA that refract and reflect the grace of God and give off a variety of hews of holiness.

Some of us receive abilities to serve others with massive compassion; others are able to give with extravagant generosity. Peter's point is to recognize that each of us received *something*, and whatever we have received, use it to the glory of God.

There are sides to God's attributes that are not obviously visible to the world without a life for them to flow through. Grace and truth lived out in time and space give application whereas truth only written in two dimensions is difficult to grasp. This is one of the most dramatic ways that God demonstrates who He is to a world gone dark. As ordinary people become filled with God and willingly make themselves available to use their time, talents, and treasures to serve others, the world cannot help but stand back wondering what this all means.

One of the truths I have come to understand is that gifts are two-sided coins. On one side of the coin we enjoy using what God has given us. But on the other side, when we are seen alive in God and passionately utilizing what we have been given, it opens others up to see God present in a way that they maybe never have.

As a pastor of a thriving church, one of my greatest joys is seeing hundreds of people serving one another in an effort to create an environment in which people who are far from Christ can come into our church services and encounter God. I love to see artists creating things, baristas making coffee art, mechanically inclined people (I am so grateful for people like this since I am impaired in this arena) fixing and redesigning buildings, musicians bringing us into the presence of God during worship—so many different giftings, all working together to testify to the wisdom and majesty of God.

It is a very humbling thing to walk the hallways of my church early on Sunday morning and see so many people praying, preparing, and willingly using what God has given them to bless others. This is such a powerful way to portray grace and truth with our gifts. We are all different in our gifting and perspectives, and it is this variety that was God's intention all along—not that only one type of gift would be celebrated more than others, but that we would complement each other. Like pieces to a jigsaw puzzle, we would together paint a complete and compelling picture.

It doesn't just have to be limited to church buildings or church services. It should be the daily focus of our lives—to steward wisely what God has given us, all for the glory of God. All so that we can lift up someone's gaze long enough to see through our lives that there is a God who knows them and values them.

Unfortunately we can also believe the lie that tries to tell us that we are not special, that we don't have anything to offer others. We shelve our abilities, or worse, we reserve them for our own benefit and refuse to share them. This is what Jesus told us not to do. Don't hide them under a basket. Don't extinguish them. Don't compare yourself to others and become discouraged. Every person has a gift, and each of us has a lamp stand that God has set us in. If we will use what He has given us, we will bring light and beauty to our world.

This is an "upside down" concept that we are talking about. In the world's way of doing things, it's all about leveraging what we have in order to gain more for ourselves or take what belongs to someone else. This is not the Jesus way or the kingdom path. Jesus told us that if we want to be great in His kingdom, we would have to take the servant's role. When the church passionately cares for others, gives to others, and serves others with nothing asked in return, the door opens for Jesus, the ultimate servant, to be seen without distraction or distortion.

OUR WORDS

Our words are more powerful than we can imagine. The Bible says that our words have the power to give life and healing or to inflict death and damage (Prov. 18:21). The words we speak are by nature spiritual, and even though we forget about much of what we say, those words continue to float through the universe, and perhaps more importantly, they stick in the hearts and souls of the people who hear them.

If you were to think back over various moments of your life, you would probably be able to remember something that someone said or didn't say to you that affected you a significant way. I can personally recall several pivotal moments in my life when I received encouragement from someone who went out of their way to do so. There have been many times when I have faced discouragement and felt ready to give up that a few of those words came back to me and reinvigorated my soul to keep going. I am so grateful for the encouragers in my life. There have been other times when the exact opposite occurred. It's amazing to me how just one negative word or one critical e-mail takes the wind out of you. Words affect us at the deepest core of our being. If we are going to be people who reflect the goodness and wisdom of God, we are then going to be people who learn to use words to build up and not tear down.

Paul wrote to the Christians at Colosse about the connection between our words and the release of God's grace through us to those who are far from God.

> Walk in wisdom toward outsiders, making the best use of the time. Let your speech always be gracious, seasoned with salt, so that you may know how you ought to answer each person.
>
> —Colossians 4:5–6

This idea of our words and the way we communicate being likened to the affect of salt is an echo of Jesus's words in the Sermon on the Mount. When He laid out the mission and modus operandi of the church to be the "light of the word," He also compared the affect that the church would have as "salt" that would season this darkened world with God flavors. Grace and mercy are not the preferred seasoning of a self-centered, "me-first" world, but it is in the kingdom of God. Christians are set in this dying world not just to be a subculture but to be a prophetic mouthpiece, living in the truth and speaking the truth, but all the while having our words and actions full of the salt of grace.

We take salt for granted in our culture because it is so readily available and added to everything. In ancient times salt was a valuable commodity that represented life and covenant. Salt was often rare and very expensive, but extremely necessary for daily life. Salt was and is still used for seasoning and flavoring. It was also used for thousands of years to be a preservative. It kept food from breaking down and becoming spoiled. It's also known that our bodies need a certain amount of salt in our bodies to live. Salt will also make you thirsty. This is what Paul and Jesus had in mind for kingdom people—that we use our words to release grace and to create a thirst for God by the words we use.

Thirst is one of life's most powerful desires. There are also degrees of how thirsty we are. If you have ever gone without water for an entire day (such a complete fast), you know what thirst can do to you. It begins to control your every thought, and you will stop at nothing to get a drink. A question we should ask ourselves is, "Does the way that I communicate create thirst in others to want to know more about God, or do my words leave a bad taste in their mouths?"

Jesus was the ultimate communication of God the Father to the world. That's why He is called the eternal "word" of God. It is interesting to read the Gospels with this in mind. Jesus didn't mince words when teaching the truth. But He also had a way with His words that arrested people's attention, even when the subject matter was corrective or controversial. People were willing to drop everything at the rumor of His presence in a location. They sat spellbound, listening to every word He had to say. Why? Because Jesus was perfectly truth and grace.

Grace as a virtue is otherworldly, or better put, other-kingdom-ly. It values others, it forgives, and it offers hope and meaning. That's the message exemplified in Jesus, and it must become our attitude and virtue. Our words are powerful tools of grace to build up others in a world that loves to deconstruct ideas and people with words set on fire.

It is unfortunate that the church as a whole has become so well known for defending what we believe as biblically true but doing it without a spirit of graciousness and compassion. If we could see the opportunities around us each day as open doors to preserve and season the world, we would not be able to keep people away from the church. It is equally important that the church become known as a community of grace as much as we have emphasized ourselves being people of truth. We now need a revolution in our words. Grace is the language of heaven and if we are going to truly be citizens of a heavenly kingdom, we need to start speaking the language and demonstrating the culture. This is what it means to color our world.

Chapter 5

PEOPLE FROM THE FUTURE

You're here because you know something. What you know you can't explain, but you feel it. You've felt it your entire life, that there's something wrong with the world.[1]

—MORPHEUS

LAST YEAR A friend forwarded an odd but interesting article to me from a British online magazine about a man who mysteriously showed up in Switzerland at the famed Large Hadron Collider near Geneva. The gigantic supercollider is world famous for its groundbreaking research on subatomic particles and their relationship to the formation of the universe. Thousands of scientists have been involved in research at this underground laboratory developing hypotheses about parallel universes, dark mass, and nuclear energy. Many experts believe the work done here will help scientist unlock the mysteries of the universe.

Apparently this young man claimed to be from the future, sent back in time to keep them from destroying the entire world through their experimentation. This oddly dressed young man believed that what they were doing in the supercollider was detrimental to the future health of Planet Earth. He spoke about what the future looked like in strange detail. He said there were no national borders in the future, and there was limitless power available for everyone as well as unlimited KIT KAT candy bars. (This sounds like my kind of future!) The story claims that he was taken into custody by Swiss officials while trying to gather fuel from their garbage bins for his time machine that strikingly resembled a small kitchen appliance. He was supposedly placed in an observation cell within a psychiatric unit, from which he later seemed to disappear. He must've found a way back to the future!

This story, like so many others that we have heard throughout our lifetime about people from the future, traversing time to warn us of what is to come, is most likely a hoax (call me an optimist) fabricated for entertainment value and published with sarcasm. We love to theorize about the future and what it will be like with its fashions, technology, and progress. We ponder whether the world will be a better place, safer and more humane, or whether it will be worse off than it is now. The future can hold both excitement and anticipation or fear and trepidation, depending upon where you are viewing the future.

What if I were to tell you that there are people from the future living here, right now? What if I were to tell you that these people, from the future, are here to prepare the world for what is to come and are living fueled by a never-ending power source from their native dimension? Would you believe me or dismiss me as a fiction-writing storyteller on par with those tabloid, tongue-in-cheek news agencies? What if I were to tell you that you are possibly from the future? If you have been born again by the Spirit of God, then you are a part of the community of the kingdom, and you truly are a person from the future!

The church is described as aliens and strangers, not at home in this world's system that is passing away right before our eyes. We have been translated from one kingdom into another, from darkness into the light of day. We are empowered by the Holy Spirit and experiencing eternal life now. We are citizens of a kingdom that has indeed been inaugurated victoriously but is yet still on its way. Our feet are planted on earth, but our hearts are enthroned with Christ in the heavenly realms.

> For you are a chosen people. You are royal priests, a holy nation, God's very own possession. As a result, you can show others the goodness of God, for he called you out of the darkness into his wonderful light. "Once you had no identity as a people; now you are God's people. Once you received no mercy; now you have received God's mercy." Dear friends, I warn you as "temporary residents and foreigners."
>
> —1 PETER 2:9–11, NLT

We have been placed in the midst of this world as the forerunners of the future, here in anticipation of the fullness of the kingdom that will ultimately come when Jesus returns. We are a prophetic announcement of the new day that is dawning right in the midst of the old.

If we look back to Genesis, we remember that from the very beginning God ordained that *the night* precedes *the day* in His original model for creation (Gen. 1:5). Between the darkness of the night and the full light of noonday comes a brief overlap when it is not any longer dark but not yet fully light. We call this time of day "twilight," and this is where we live as the church, at threshold of the Day of the Lord. Even though it seems at times that the world is getting darker, we see evidence that the day is already shining within His people, the church.

This new day dawned very early on a Sunday morning, when Jesus vacated the tomb and death itself was left behind in His wake. What Jesus began at His own resurrection will reach its zenith when the gospel is finally made known to all nations and the world that Jesus won back and His people welcome His glorious return to this earth to finally be restored and healed.

We are the firstfruits of Jesus's reward. We are residents between the times in an age that is passing away, anticipating the one that is to come. We exist in the in-between and the overlap of two eras, living from and for the future. We are the first light breaking across the horizon of a world in transition.

> The darkness is passing away and the true light is already shining.
>
> —1 John 2:8

We are those who are walking in the light of God's truth. The light that reveals things the way they truly are. The light that exposes what lies ahead on the path. We are here to pull the blinders off of a blindfolded world and debunk the delusion that the devil has used to keep them from the God who loves them. We are called to live in such a way that those who are still under false assumption will know that no one other than Jesus is King.

Remember how Jesus taught us to pray? "Your kingdom come, your will be done, on earth as it is in heaven" (Matt. 6:10–11). I propose that He also intended us to pray this prophetically and live out the implications of this prayer as well. He wanted us to live and pray in full expectation that God's coming reign and rule on earth is not just wishful thinking but an inevitable reality. He wanted us to be people who are not moved by the day-to-day shifting of this present world but live from the future reality, here in the present actuality, each of us working to see His will done on earth beginning here and now, in us and through us.

The church is called to be a prophetic sign post for the world, boldly pointing back at what God has done in the finished work of Jesus upon the cross and expectantly pointing forward in time to what lies ahead. As the world beholds us, His church, it should seem strangely odd to them because we are so "other-worldly" in the way we live and order our priorities. We are here as a sneak peak of coming attractions of the coming age, giving a visible demonstration of those intentions. We are proclaiming the presence and the power of the king, not just in the days of the past, but also here right now. Jesus is the hope of the future and that future lives in us. We are people from the future!

THE PRESENCE OF THE FUTURE

Jesus came to the earth at a time when there were multiple viewpoints of how the kingdom of God would come. Some of the most ardent scholars believed it was the coming of Messiah that would lead to the immediate overthrow of all Israel's enemies and reestablishment of the glory of Israel's identity. When the kingdom came, it would be a miraculous fulfillment of all the prophets had declared. God would once and for all establish His rule and reign in the earth and eradicate all evil and death. He would reverse all that is wrong in this sin-ridden world and make it right once again. This was their hope for the future.

They saw history broken into two epochs: the present age and what they came to identify as the age to come. They believed that the present age was marked by darkness, sin, disease, and death. They saw in the future age to come that God would reverse all that was wrong with this broken world, restoring it back to its original order with Israel at the center of God's global government. Heaven and earth would once again be united under the enthroned Messiah.

This long-anticipated Savior-King would one day suddenly appear in the temple according to the prophets, reveal Himself, and lead all of God's people (Israel) in the overthrow of their enemies and finally reorder everything the way it was supposed to be. As part of this fulfillment, certain long-awaited promises were anticipated. The resurrection of the dead, judgment of Gentile nations, and the restoring of creation itself would all occur in this hoped for "age to come." As the Anglican scholar N. T. Wright often phrases it, "the final putting-to-rights of all things."[2]

The Pharisees, the theological descendants of the military commander and revolutionary Jonathan Macabee, were looking for something even a bit more dramatic to indicate that the kingdom was finally here. They had developed a litmus test and a timeline of sorts to identify and qualify any potential candidate Messiah—signs that God had finally sent "the one" who would set in motion their eschatological hopes and expectations. They assumed that when this future did come, it would be bloody, revolutionary, and a miraculous moment leading to political promotion for them and validation for their interpretation of the Torah.

Jesus began His ministry with a strikingly bold announcement. Shortly after His baptism and temptation, Jesus began declaring that the kingdom of God was here, *right now,* in their midst and available for all men and women to experience.

> From that time Jesus began to preach and to say, "Repent, for the kingdom of heaven is at hand."
>
> —MATTHEW 4:17, NKJV

This was a radical departure from what the Pharisees were expecting. He didn't first go to the religious leaders and scholars and seek their affirmation or approval. In fact, while Jesus was welcoming sinners and outsiders into the kingdom, He made radical statements seemingly excluding those who considered themselves caretakers of God's throne. He didn't bow to their pressure or attempt to fit in with their movement. Jesus told them He had come from heaven and that the Father had sent Him—that in Him the future was now breaking into the present and that the world as they knew it was shifting right in front of their eyes. It would take a complete change of mind and thinking for them to be able to see it and enter it.

> Truly, I say to you, the tax collectors and the prostitutes go into the kingdom of God before you. For John came to you in the way of righteousness, and you did not believe him, but the tax collectors and the prostitutes believed him. And even when you saw it, you did not afterward change your minds and believe him.
>
> —MATTHEW 21:31–32

The Pharisees were unable to see it. Their perceptions blinded them from realizing that all of their hopes for the age to come were standing right in front of them in flesh and blood. Jesus had come to His own, but His own did not recognize Him. They were unwilling to receive the kingdom because they didn't understand that it could be anything other than bloody, political, and ultimately futuristic. As George Eldon Ladd, the New Testament scholar, described, this was a mystery to them:

> The new truth, now given to men by revelation in the person and mission of Jesus, is that the Kingdom which is to come finally in apocalyptic power, as foreseen by Daniel, has in fact entered into the world in advance in a hidden form to work secretly within and among men.[3]

Jesus was declaring to the world that the power of the future age that they were all waiting for had *now* broken into history and was already at work. Heaven had invaded earth with the presence of the future. The kingdom was indeed here now, even if not yet fully realized. This was a revolutionary idea. Jesus had initiated the kingdom, the reign and rule of God in the earth, but would not consummate it until His future return in glory.

This imminent kingdom that dealt first with the heart and would work its way out into the world was an offense to the religious establishment. They were looking for Jesus to sign off on their legalistic approach to living out their faith, but instead they were confronted with wisdom that astounded them. At every turn they were left speechless as Jesus taught with an authority that they had never witnessed, worked miracles and healings that were unexplainable, and set town after town on fire with messianic fervor. The Sadducees and Pharisees responded to Jesus the way that perhaps we would respond to someone claiming to be from the future. "This guy has lost His mind!" They could not wrap their minds around what He was claiming.

> Now when He was asked by the Pharisees when the kingdom of God would come, He answered them and said, "The kingdom of God does not come with observation; nor will they say 'See here!' or 'See there!' For indeed, the kingdom of God is within you."
>
> —LUKE 17:20–21, NKJV

Jesus came as one from the future. He operated out of the knowledge and power of the kingdom that was here now but not yet complete. It wasn't that He functioned on a pro-rated anointing or scaled-down version of the kingdom of God. It was incomplete only in its application and finality.

He was here to set off a chain reaction that would fulfill the story that had long ago begun with Abraham and now was going to culminate in His own sacrificial death and resurrection. This was the day when all of the blessings that had only been associated with the hope of the age to come would collide with this present dark world. Heaven had broken into history in the person of Jesus Christ. The future had emerged from the tomb on that resurrection morning, and things would never be the same.

MARKED BY HOPE

Jesus indicated that the Holy Spirit's presence upon Him was the mark of authentication that the kingdom was truly present and active. It was the anointing of the Holy Spirit upon Him that enabled Him to overthrow the works of darkness and overthrow satanic powers. Just as the Spirit of God had hovered over the face of the waters at the dawn of God's first creative acts, He was now present upon Jesus, the eternal Word of God, as He was inaugurating a new genesis. The demonstration of healing and deliverance over demonic powers was an indicator that the future expectation of salvation, deliverance, and healing was now happening. All that had been hoped for was now available. The message of the kingdom was *good news* because it brought the first light of hope the world had ever seen.

> But if it is by the finger of God that I cast out demons,
> then the kingdom of God has come upon you.
>
> —LUKE 11:20

The gospel that Jesus preached was primarily a message of hope. The same hope that most had put off until a future, eschatological time was now being proclaimed and demonstrated right before their eyes. The gospel was a call to repent or change the way we see ourselves in light of what God was now doing and to believe in Jesus as our only hope for freedom from sin's bondage and our resulting brokenness. Their future hopes had arrived today, and if they would only believe, freedom was imminent.

Those who believed and followed Jesus became the building blocks of what He would construct to form His kingdom community, the church, a redeemed remnant from this present, dark, and dying world who are already experiencing eternal life and living from the future backward—a people who are marked by hope.

> Who have tasted the heavenly gift, and have shared in the Holy Spirit, and have tasted the goodness of the word of God and the powers of the age to come.
>
> —Hebrews 6:4–5

The writer of Hebrews describes the church as those who have "tasted the goodness of the powers of the age to come." That perfectly describes what happens when we are born again by the Spirit of God. All that seems impossible in a world flawed and broken becomes a reality in the hearts of God's people by faith. When we trust in Jesus as the true King of this world, His kingdom comes and we receive in advance the down payment of peace, joy, love, and hope that is presently not native in this world.

Paul describes this gift of the Holy Spirit as a "seal" or "mark" that God has placed within our hearts as a down payment or earnest deposit of our entire redemption that we will receive when Jesus returns and brings heaven and earth together finally. (See Ephesians 1:13–14.) At that time He will resurrect our dead bodies, and death will be no more. He will banish Satan and all of his minions, and there will be no more sin or temptation. There will be no more war, injustice, racism, or poverty. Mothers will never cry again for their lost children. Guilt will never again tarnish the hearts of God's people. Shame will finally be silenced. This is the hope that all of creation is longing and groaning to see right now. It is this hope that has already become a reality ahead of time to those of us who by faith enter into this kingdom now.

> For the earnest expectation of creation eagerly waits for the revealing of the sons of God. For the creation was subjected to futility, not willingly, but because of Him who subjected it in hope; because the creation itself also will be delivered from the bondage of corruption into the glorious liberty of the children of God. For we know that the whole creation groans and labors with birth pangs together until now. Not only that, but we also who have the firstfruits of the Spirit, even we ourselves groan within ourselves, eagerly waiting for the adoption, the redemption of our body. For we were saved in this hope, but hope that is seen is not hope; for why does one still hope for what he sees? But if we hope for what we do not see, we eagerly wait for it with perseverance.
>
> —ROMANS 8:19–25, NKJV

What this means for us is that in spite of the fact that the kingdom of God has not come in its fullness, we are carriers of and witnesses to its presence now. The kingdom is here, Jesus said it, and we have experienced it. The hope that had always been held out for the future has arrived now, and we are forever marked and sealed by it. While we wait for the finality of it, we can already begin to work and live as if it is here already. Hope is our motivator. Whatever we are hoping for, we will work toward. If we have found our hope in what Jesus began at His resurrection, we must also invest our lives working toward what He has promised to bring to pass upon His return.

To live in a world that is primarily ruled and marked by fear is an opportunity for the church to operate from a spirit of faith, hope, and love and a holy confidence and boldness that stand out above all despair. When you know what the future holds, you don't have to be shaken every time the economy shifts. We don't have to become frustrated with the political systems or fearful of epidemics ending history. We know where the future is going. We know how this all ends—and begins again. We know whose government is going to thrive and who's going to be in charge when it's all said and done. We have more than a hunch; we have hope. We don't just give our best guess as to what the future holds. We are those who are held by the One who holds the future. The future already is living and active inside us, and we are indelibly marked by it.

We are the people of God, the sons of the kingdom, who are the colony of heaven, formed by the Holy Spirit, living as light in the country of the dead.[4] Jesus has sent us ahead of His appearing to establish the culture of the kingdom here. We are people from the future.

COLONY OF HEAVEN

The concept of colonization is as old as human kingdoms. Large empires conquer smaller states or cities by force and then saturate them with their own unique culture. Many of the empires you read about in your Bible such as Egypt, Babylon, Greece, and especially Rome had a colonization strategy. The Roman Empire had succeeded in conquering most of the Mediterranean world by the time Jesus and the church appeared on history's stage and had, in most cases, succeeded in transplanting Roman culture throughout.

One major example of colonization is the city of Philippi,

named after Philip, the father of Alexander the Great. At one point the city had been the location of a decisive victory for Caesar Augustus (then called Octavian) over Brutus and Cassius, the conspirators against Julius Caesar. As a reward to the city, Augustus had the city renovated into a Roman motif and gave them rights and privileges that only citizens of the great city Rome itself possessed. The inhabitants of Philippi considered themselves Romans and were very proud of their citizenship. The empire considered Philippi a colony to which they transplanted Roman citizens, retired military heroes, and reproduced Roman culture with the intention that it would spread to the surrounding region. The idea came out of the necessity to transmit the culture and language of the empire into conquered lands in order to unify the people and expand their cultural influence.

As the apostle Paul traveled and established churches throughout the width and the breadth of the Roman Empire, he would've been fully aware of this practice of colonization. He would often point to cultural icons such as war garb, political phrases, and word pictures common to his readers to illustrate kingdom realities. Many of the terms and illustrations Paul employed in his epistles to describe the church's role in the world are right out of Roman or Greek culture, especially the idea of citizenship and colonization.

One such example of this is found in Philippians 3:20–21:

> But our citizenship is in heaven, and from it we await a Savior, the Lord Jesus Christ, who will transform our lowly body to be like his glorious body, by the power that enables him even to subject all things to himself.

Paul is making the point that as Christians our true citizenship is in the kingdom of God. We are citizens, a colony of the future kingdom, whom God has placed in the world to influence (salt) and demonstrate the will (light) of our King now. We are ambassadors sent ahead to represent our King, prepare the way for Him, and to live from the values, power, and truth of the future age in the here and now. We are people caught living in this present age, motivated and fully aware of what is breaking in. We know how this all shakes out. We know who wins; we know who is already reigning. We have experienced the power of salvation already. We are living in the midst of a broken creation as a born-again forerunner of the new creation.

N. T. Wright, a leading New Testament scholar, relates it this way:

> From one point of view, the day has already dawned, while from another it's still on it's way.... He is like someone taking off just as dawn is breaking and flying rapidly westward, catching up with the end of the night and arriving in the new country in time to experience dawn all over again. His body and mind know it's already daytime, while the world around him is still waiting for the dawn to break. That is the picture of the Christian, living in the new day of God's kingdom—a kingdom launched by Jesus— while the rest of the world is still turning over in bed.[5]

One of my favorite movies growing up in the 1980s was *Back to the Future.* You may recall Michael J. Fox playing the role of Marty McFly, a young man who goes back in time with the help of a Einstein-like scientist and a time-traveling Delorean equipped with a flux capacitor. One of the most memorable scenes of the movie is when he shows up at the high school prom dance where his mother and father are supposed fall in love. There comes a moment when Marty takes matters into his own hands and jumps up onto the stage to fill in for the guitar player in order to make sure that destiny happens the way it's supposed to. It works, and his shy, teenage father finally dances with his mom, and romance finally sparks. With the pressure off he decides to show off and introduces the audience to rock 'n' roll and a song that would later be made famous by Chuck Berry. He tells the audience that the song he's about to play is an "oldie" where he comes from, even though it has never been played before. He gives instructions to the rest of the band and tells them, "Watch me for the changes, and try to keep up!"[6]

The crowd and band just stand there looking at him strangely for a moment because they have never seen or heard anything like this before. But after a few moments the band goes all in, and the crowd begins to dance to this new song from the future. He had introduced them to something they didn't know existed and had never heard before. He brought the future to them.

I can't help but see the church in this light. We are people from the future. We know what the future holds and who holds it. We don't live out of fear but in faith—a faith that is anchored in the knowledge that we are not alone, steering this big blue marble through space, but that God is in the process of making all things new.

We aren't looking for a way to return to the good ol' days; we are looking forward in time to that day when everything is put under His feet. We live here, but we are importing the culture of our homeland. Our language is seasoned with grace, we are clothed with humility and the armor of light, and our allegiance is to the King who has vanquished the ultimate enemy of sin and death. We are resident aliens, colonizing the world with the values and ethics of the kingdom of God.

We must see ourselves this way. We are those who have traded in our passport from the land of the darkness in exchange for one that is "in Christ. We have buried the old man and been resurrected into the newness of life, complete with the rights and privileges of the citizens of heaven. We are new creations, the first of what God is doing and intends to complete. We are foreigners in a strange land, sent to "heavenize" the earth.

Eugene Peterson describes this conviction of what the role of the church is:

> The short answer that I had come to embrace through the years of my pastoral formation...is that the Holy Spirit forms church to be a colony of heaven in the country of death....Church is a core element in the strategy of the Holy Spirit for providing human witness and physical presence to the Jesus-inaugurated kingdom of God in this world. It is not that kingdom complete, but it is that kingdom.[7]

CULTURES IN TENSION

If you have ever traveled outside of the United States, you know how different cultures can be. I have traveled all over the world and have seen the variety of cultures and peoples from the masses of humanity in Sao Paulo, Brazil, to the remote corners of India. I am consistently awed by the vast differences and variety in culture and way of life that each place and people group have. The difference between the culture of the kingdom of God and the culture of this world are polar opposite.

The cultures of this fallen world are founded on men's failed attempts to gather colonies of people around faulty causes and values that ultimately lead anywhere but up. Beginning with Babel and culminating in the Book of Revelation with Babylon the Great, man's best attempts only bring more darkness and hopelessness. The colony that Jesus is building on the earth is called the church. His "called out and unto a purpose" people are carriers of the DNA of God's kingdom. We bring the language of grace and hope to a world whose mother tongue is despair and selfishness. We live loyal to the King who is already reigning even though He is unseen, declaring and demonstrating the power and presence of the kingdom. We have been called to live presently from the reality of the coming kingdom, empowered and established by the finished work of Christ in the past.

The world is not on a collision course to destruction but rather a bringing together of all things under the authority of the true King, Jesus Christ. The Mayans were wrong; 2012 is not the end of the world (especially since by the time you are reading this, 2012 is a distant memory). The world is God's, and He is not abandoning it; He is committed to restoring it. A new heaven and a new earth will both be brought under the lordship of Jesus. We, as the church, will rule over everything with Him when it is all said and done.

> ...and seated him [Jesus] at his right hand in the heavenly places, far above all rule and authority and power and dominion, and above every name that is named, not only in this age but also in the one to come. And he put all things under his feet and gave him as head over all things to the church, which is his body, the fullness of him who fills all in all.
>
> —EPHESIANS 1:20–23

The ends of the ages have converged at one place and one time within history—the cross and resurrection of Jesus Christ. The old age with its dominion was crucified and the new world was inaugurated through the resurrection. We are people ahead of our time. Stanley Hauerwas, theologian and ethicist from Duke University, says it well:

> Square one is that colony made up of those who are special, different, alien and distinctive only in the sense that they are those who have heard Jesus say "Follow me," and have come forth to be a part of a new people, a colony formed by hearing his invitation and saying yes.[8]

The culture of heaven is one that is ever increasing and growing brighter, and populated by a people who believe and enter the kingdom of God by faith—people who are living by the constitution and declaration of dependence upon the government of God. This is the church that Jesus is building.

The word *church* is used by Jesus twice in the Gospels and is used repetitively in Acts and the Epistles. It was originally a classical Greek word *ekklesia,* which means "a group or assembly of persons called together for a particular purpose."[9] It was adopted to describe the people of God living in the present culture. Historically the word was used of the political body of citizens living within a certain city. In times when a new city was being established or assimilated into the conquering empire's culture, a group of citizens would convene to discuss and decide upon legislation or policy. This specific group within the overall population was referred to as "the *ekklesia*" or "the church." This perfectly describes the role of the church within society who are the "light of the world" and the "salt of the earth."

When the church of Jesus gathers together in worship, boldly declares the Word of God, and enters into true *koinonia* fellowship, we are reaffirming Jesus's rightful reign and rule over our lives, cities, and the nations. In that environment God is enthroned and His kingdom has come (Ps. 22:3). When we pray "thy kingdom come, thy will be done," we are legislating and enforcing the agenda of heaven. We are a culture within a culture, leaven that is permeating the whole lump. We are the seed that is sown and bringing forth good fruit. We are the light that is shining in the midst of a world gone dark. We are the radiant church that Jesus is preparing to reign and rule with Him. We may not know the future, but we do know Jesus, and the future is summed up in Him. If we know Jesus, we know the future.

What does it mean to be people who are already experiencing the present reign of Jesus as King but yet living in a world that hasn't? It means that we must be fully aware and fully loyal to the kingdom of God even while we are living behind enemy lines. We are to work as if His kingdom is already here, because in earnest it already is. We are importing the truth from the future into this present evil age. This is what it means to "shine bright."

> Do all things without grumbling or disputing, that you may be blameless and innocent, children of God without blemish in the midst of a crooked and twisted generation, among whom you shine as lights in the world, holding fast to the word of life, so that in the day of Christ I may be proud that I did not run in vain or labor in vain.
>
> —PHILIPPIANS 2:14–16

We should not be alarmed when the way we conduct our lives stands in stark contrast to those around us. That's what light does: it draws contrast and enhances definition. Our presence and practice in this world is a sure sign that the long night of sin's and death's dominion is being folded up and put away. The church should be a glaring reminder that something has changed. The world is not as it was and will not be left as it is. This way of living is prophetic because it originates outside of this world, not simply conforming to the pattern of this world. We are not defined by the fear of the unknown, but we have a holy confidence because we know how this turns out. If there is anything to fear, it should be that somehow, in our ignorance or apathy, we would remain indistinguishable from the world, a lamp put under a basket that is kept hidden. The kingdom of God has exploded into history first through Jesus and now through His body. As we live wisely in this age, our kingdom-building lifestyles will serve as lamp posts that line the road, leading others who are lost to find the truth.

SECTION 2

BE THE DIFFERENCE

I N THIS NEXT section we are going to bring into focus what it means for each of us as disciples of Jesus to live as light in the midst of a world gone dark. We are going to put skin on the concepts that we have laid out in the first section and lay out what it looks like to *be the difference.* Long before we can make a difference, we have to make a decision to be the difference ourselves. This is what it means to be the light of the world and the salt of the earth. This is what it means to be radiant.

Ours is a holy calling, given to us before the foundations of the world, to stand up and stand out in an intentional and Spirit-driven way.

> Therefore do not be ashamed of the testimony of our Lord, nor of me His prisoner, but share with me in the sufferings for the gospel according to the power of God, who has saved us and called us with a holy calling, not according to our works, but according to

His own purpose and grace which was given to us in
Christ Jesus before time began.

—2 TIMOTHY 1:8–10, NKJV

We are called to good works that flow from a life fueled
by vision and supernatural grace and power. It starts with
us. Jesus has called us, saved us, filled us, and positioned us
as lamps upon lamp stands, all with the intention to "give
light" to the place where He has stationed us. We are not to
fear but to shine and be captivated by a compelling vision for
the affect our lives, families, and churches can make as we
live lives of passion for the cause of Christ fueling our hearts.

We do not wage war with the weapons of the flesh or
walk in the same way that the masses are traveling. We
don't implement the values of a world gone dark that has
been tried and found wanting. We are called to live by the
genetic code of the kingdom of God and to order our lives
in such a way that we become a clear and understandable
expression of the kingdom of God. Our lives should be like
a giant movie screen that displays the wisdom and grace of
God upon us for the world's audience to view.

It's time for each of us to embrace our true identity and
unashamedly live empowered by the Holy Spirit, giving
witness to the truth. A return to the values found in the
primitive but powerful days of the church as it emerged
as an alternative community in the Book of Acts is badly
needed. In order to move forward, we must go back in time
to where the future first emerged on the scene.

The following chapters will lay out five specific strands of
spiritual mitochondria for what it means to be radiant. My
prayer is that as we explore each of them, the Holy Spirit will
imbed these core convictions deeply within our souls.

Chapter 6

BE WORD CENTERED:
IN SHIFTING TIMES

The Bible is not an end in itself, but a means to bring
men to an intimate and satisfying knowledge of
God, that they may enter into Him, that they may
delight in His Presence, may taste and know the
inner sweetness of the very God Himself in the core
and center of their hearts.[1]

—A. W. TOZER

But he answered, "It is written, 'Man shall not live by
bread alone, but by every word that comes from the
mouth of God.'"

—MATTHEW 4:4

JESUS HAD JUST gone public in the waters of the
Jordan River, baptized by John and anointed with the
Holy Spirit. The voice of His heavenly Father fully
affirmed Him as His "beloved Son" and propelled Him into
messianic ministry in the sight of all of Israel. Before He
preached one sermon, performed one miracle, or called His
first disciple, Jesus was led out into the Judean wilderness to
pass the test of temptation.

Retracing the steps of Moses leading the children of Israel
out of their Egyptian bondage and through the wilderness
for forty years, Jesus was in the wilderness for forty days.
Hungry, thirsty, and weakened physically and spiritually,
Jesus was confronted by the devil at His weakest moment.

The wilderness testing had been the downfall of the

generation that had experienced a miraculous deliverance out of Egypt. They had turned their backs on God when their hunger and thirst had gotten to be too much. They were willing to give up their inheritance for the onions and leeks of their former life. They had disdain for the provision of manna, the miraculous bread from heaven, sent to them daily during their sojourning. Now doubt and bitterness had replaced the joy and celebration that had once marked them as God's firstborn people on the deliverance side of the Red Sea parting. They had come right up to the edge of the Promised Land and spied it out from across the Jordan, but they were intimidated by the size of the enemies awaiting them. In their fear they had forgotten who they were and the presence and promise of God for them.

Now Jesus was wandering the hills of scorched sand and facing the same difficult temptations that had faced the people of Israel long ago and all of us today. He too would spy out, not only the land of Israel but also all the kingdoms of the world by supernatural transport. He was offered a shortcut to His destiny by the cunning deceiver: "All these I will give you, if you will fall down and worship me" (Matt. 4:7). He was encouraged to take matters into His own hands and turn the hard rocks into bread—an invitation to satisfy Himself with situational sustenance and bypass the painful effects of fasting. Instead Jesus responded to the devil with the Word of God that was strengthening Him and feeding His soul, "Man shall not live by bread alone, but by every word that comes from the mouth of God" (Matt. 4:4).

The point? Jesus was making it clear that regardless of the circumstances or difficulties we find ourselves in, the real source of our life is found in the feast of God's Word. Food may feed our flesh and nourish us physically for a moment, but real life is found in hearing and understanding God's voice as spoken through His Word to us. To value anything else more or place anything else above God's Word as the authority and center of our lives will truly end in an unfulfilled and unsatisfied existence.

HAS GOD SAID?

The Word of God has been at the center of satanic attack since the very beginning of time. God's Word is the source of life and truth, the sustaining force of the entire universe and the way that God has revealed Himself and His will. In order to overthrow or thwart an all-powerful God who is beyond defeat, the only alternative for an archenemy to gain an advantage is to challenge communication to a weaker, more vulnerable partner and to call into question the validity, the importance, or the rightness of what God has said so that access can be gained by the gap of doubt and unbelief.

He tried it with Jesus during His temptation experience, and he will use it against you and me, rest assured. He challenged what God had openly stated about Jesus in front of the whole world, that He was indeed God's one and only beloved Son, in whom He was well pleased. He waited until the moment when those words were weeks in the past and the present circumstances were wearing on Jesus's mind and body before appealing to Him and calling those words of God into question. "If you are the son of God...." (vv. 3, 5). For Jesus to pick up a rock and turn it to bread in order to prove His sonship would have been an act invalidating the Word that was already at work within Him, sustaining Him in His purpose and obedience to the Father.

This is Satan's only effective tactic in the war against God and His people. As long as there is agreement and faith between God and man, there is nothing that is impossible. The god of this world has no creative power of his own, just the twisting tools of manipulation and deception. Unfortunately it was this tactic that worked in the beginning to create a breech in the heaven/earth unity and bring humanity out from under the protective shelter of obedience into full exposure and death. The serpent called into question what God had clearly communicated as true and right, knowing that if the first seed of doubt and independence could find fertile soil in the mind of God's regent of the earth, the ensuing division would bring death and create a void of darkness for him to operate in and gain dominion.

> Now the serpent was more crafty than any other beast of the field that the LORD God had made. He said to the woman, "Did God actually say, 'You shall not eat of any tree in the garden'?" And the woman said to the serpent, "We may eat of the fruit of the trees in the garden, but God said, 'You shall not eat of the fruit of the tree that is in the midst of the garden, neither shall you touch it, lest you die.'" But the serpent said to the woman, "You will not surely die. For God knows that when you eat of it your eyes will be opened, and you will be like God, knowing good and evil."
>
> —GENESIS 3:1–5

Satan has operated this way throughout every age of time in history and still operates by this methodology today. He takes full advantage of our spiritual blindness and sinful nature and uses our wounded hearts against us, still calling into question the validity or veracity of God's Word in our lives. He convinces generation after generation that the hole that longs to be filled inside of us and the hunger pangs we experience can somehow be satisfied and filled by other things. He keeps us on the treadmill of deception and distraction, causing us to die a long, slow death of spiritual starvation. He understands that if we ever taste the goodness and the power of God's

Word at work in our lives, we will lose a taste for any fare this world has to offer. The Word of God is the light that alone awakens us to the truth and the grace of God.

FLASHPOINT OF REFORMATION

Historically there is a correlation between the availability and emphasis of the Bible as the Word of God and the vibrancy of the church's passion and purpose. As long as the flame of God's Word is shining bright, illuminating the body of Christ, hope remains alive and the church prevails. Remove the Bible, either by discrediting it so badly that interest is lost or by making it unavailable to the masses, and the church begins to experience weakness by a sort of spiritual anorexia. As Israel did during the times of Eli, when the word of the Lord becomes rare, our vision of God and vocation begins to grow dim. (See 1 Samuel 3:1.)

Throughout much of European history in the Middle Ages the written Word of God was unavailable to the average person. Even though most would have claimed to be "Christian," most people were unable to read. Therefore they were at the mercy of the professional clergy to know anything about God's Word. Church services were read in Latin, *making* it impossible for the listener to receive anything other than dead tradition and stale spirituality. The pope and high-level church officials had made it a capital offense for anyone to translate the Holy Scriptures of the Old and New Testaments into the common languages of the day. In their view it was too dangerous to let common people read the Bible. Only a select few were permitted to read the scarce copies of the Bible that had to be painstakingly copied by hand and kept under lock and key. Only after first spending several years learning Latin, Hebrew, and Greek was someone finally qualified and permitted to read the Bible the way that you and I take for granted today.

Think of whole generations and whole civilizations that for the most part had no idea what the Bible really had to say about anything. They were truly kept in the dark and left starving. There were no Bibles in every hotel room. There wasn't an Internet that gave people free access to the Word of God in multiple translations any time they wanted it. There was a complete blackout of the written Word of God. Having once been the home of thriving churches and passionate missionary movements, Europe was now lifeless and blind. The result of this sequestering of Scripture was a time of increased corruption and spiritual apathy that came to be known, interestingly enough, as the Dark Ages. In order for there to be any hope of rekindling the light within the church, there would need to be a miraculous alignment of circumstances and divine providence.

During the fifteenth century a young German inventor was perfecting an idea for a printing press that would utilize moveable metal typeset letters. Johannes Gutenberg had gotten the idea after studying the intricate embossment on the leather covers of his father's very costly books. Up until this time books were handwritten and painstakingly designed one at a time by skilled craftsmen and came at an extraordinary cost, and they took a very long time to produce.

His idea was to make it possible to print multiple copies of books using the same typeset over and over again. Within just a few years, after much trial and error, his idea became reality and revolutionized the availability of information throughout Europe and beyond. The first book printed upon the printing press was supposedly the famed Gutenberg Bible. Although multiple copies were made, it was still printed in Latin and unreadable to the masses. By the year 1500 it is estimated that more than twenty million books had been printed and distributed throughout

Europe. Things were changing quickly, and an even greater explosion was about to rock the continent.[2]

Martin Luther was a Catholic monk who had felt the cruelty of the darkness that pervaded his age. Attempting to find peace with God through any means possible, he even resorted to self-mortification and excessive fasting. His superior, wanting to help him move beyond his emotional despair, assigned him to biblical studies. It was while teaching through the Epistle to the Romans at the University of Wittenberg that Martin Luther discovered that his right standing before God or justification by faith was a gift that could not be earned. This became a pivotal moment in the life of the eventual reformer.

It was during this season that Martin became increasingly frustrated with what he saw as stark corruption and outright heresy within the church. He would no longer sit by and watch as indulgences were sold for the forgiveness of sin and the common man was locked out of having any knowledge of the Word of God.

On October 31, 1517, Martin Luther tacked up his Ninety-Five Theses to the door of Wittenberg Castle in protest of what he viewed as corruptions that must be addressed by the church. Within just a few short weeks copies, made on Gutenberg's printing presses, were circulating all over Europe, amplifying the voice for change and reformation.

This was the beginning of what would become known as the Protestant Reformation. The Dark Ages were coming to an end as the dawn of a new day emerged. Although there were many other leaders within the church before and during Martin Luther's time who saw the need for revival and change within the church, most were unable to bring the level of awareness to a large enough audience to see the flashpoint take spark. It was the dynamic convergence of the invention of the printing press and determined anointing upon a man such as Martin Luther that instigated a spiritual shift, altering the course of the church and the world forever.

Eventually Luther would invest his life and knowledge into translating the Bible into the German language and bringing it to every man. He befriended an English reformer, named William Tyndale, who would translate the Bible into English and eventually be burned at the stake for doing so. His famous statement to a priest was, "If God spares my life, I will cause a boy that drives the plough to know more of scripture than you do."[3] The star of the reformation was on the rise, and the Word of God was no longer hidden or held hostage.

Amazingly, since the time of the Reformation, the Word of God has revived what was once a dead and institutionalized church. Revival movements have helped restore vitality and passion to the body of Christ, and the Word of God has more availability now than it ever has. In America the average person has not one but two Bibles in his household! The Word of God has been translated into thousands of languages and dialects, bringing the truth to lands and peoples at an accelerated rate that the church has never seen in its two millennia. When the Word of God becomes the center of our focus, everything else seems to fit into perspective.

REVOLUTION OF RIGHTEOUSNESS

In the Old Testament we find another example of how the reentrance of the Word of God brings about a revolution and revival in the hearts of God's people. Josiah was the child king of Judah, who began his reign at eight years of age. As the sixteenth king of the southern kingdom he came to power at a time when the spiritual climate was at an all-time low. Idolatry and every form of wickedness and degradation had littered the landscape and the Temple Mount. Josiah was different though. Something inside drove him to seek out the God of David and return the nation back to its spiritual heritage.

In the process of restoring the temple and removing the altars and high places dedicated to the worship of false gods, a scroll that contained the Law of Moses was discovered. Most scholars believe that the Word of God had become lost over generations, and there was very little knowledge of God or His Law in Judah at this time. When it was brought before King Josiah, the words stunned him and cut straight to the heart. The Bible says that the way he responded was historic and future shifting for his nation.

> Before him there was no king like him, who turned to the Lord with all his heart and with all his soul and with all his might, according to all the Law of Moses, nor did any like him arise after him.
>
> —2 Kings 23:25

The result of this revelation brought nothing less than a revolution to Josiah's generation that affected every aspect of society. He led a rampage to rid the landscape of every idol and high place. He even had the bones of the pagan priests removed from their graves and burned along with the altars to Baal and other demonic deities that Judah had been worshipping. He rounded up all the mediums and sorcerers who taught the people to worship demons and communicate with the dead and had them executed. He was a man on a mission.

Perhaps the greatest of all of Josiah's exploits was bringing the Law, the Word of God, back to the center of Judah's cultural awareness and identity. He gathered the nation together to have it read aloud, just as it had been in Joshua's day, as a way of recommitting themselves to the covenant and purpose to which they had been unfaithful.

For the first time in generations the people of God

celebrated the feast of Passover in obedience to the commandments. A revolution was ignited as the Word of God once again gained its rightful place at the center of the lives of God's covenant people. The darkness of ignorance was now gone, and the light of truth was once again awakening a generation. The wickedness that had grown in the incubator of ignorance and neglect of God's Word by this sacred nation was dispelled in an instant as the light of truth was brought out from under the cover of deception, idolatry, and familiarity.

REDISCOVERING WHAT WE ALREADY KNOW

I wonder what would happen if we allowed the Word of God to create a similar renewal in our hearts as believers in the twenty-first-century church. What would be the outcome of rediscovering in a fresh way what we already know or think we know?

Our culture is different in many ways from the conditions of Judah during the reign of Josiah and the times of medieval Europe during the Protestant Reformation. We do not have any lack of Bibles or biblical knowledge. We have more resources, television programs, and bookstores than at any other time in history. We have hundreds of translations of the Bible available to us, and the Internet has made lack of information a relic of the past. Our culture is swarming with a million voices all competing for our attention, overloading us at the speed of fiber-optic thought. Whether it is becoming absorbed with social media or entertainment, it is so easy to find ourselves gorged on gossip and other pursuits that we give little time or attention to the most precious source of truth and food for our souls.

What we do have, however, is perhaps more devastating to our spiritual vitality and strength than lack could ever be. We have a spirit of familiarity with the Word of God.

Our disinterest has grown because we have taken it for granted, and as a result, we have grown calloused to its power and importance in our lives. While it is true that we have more access and availability to the Bible and biblical resources than ever before, ironically we tend to give less and less time and attention to the Scriptures as a valued part of our lives. It has resulted in an epidemic of biblical illiteracy within the church. Twenty-five million copies of the Bible are sold every year in America,[4] and more than 75 percent of all Americans believe that the Bible is the Word of God,[5] but somewhere there is a disconnect between availability and priority.

Sometimes we don't know what we are missing until we don't have it anymore. In other places of the world believers endure intense persecution for possessing and distributing copies of the Word of God. In China it is reported that at times in the past the Bible had become so rare that entire house churches would have a single copy or even a mere single book of the Bible that they all shared and treasured. It is held in the highest esteem. I have personally seen the eyes of Christians in third world nations fill with tears as they are handed a copy of the Bible. They are so appreciative. It is as if they were just handed a basket of food or money. To them it is of even greater value. It has gripped my heart and made me wonder about how much I take my stack of beautifully bound Bibles for granted.

The Word of God has been the centering source of stability from the very beginning. In the midst of intense persecution and growing challenges, the church constantly stayed rooted and focused by returning to the Scriptures.

And they devoted themselves to the apostles' teaching
and fellowship, to the breaking of bread and the prayers.

And awe came upon every soul, and many wonders
and signs were being done through the apostles.

—Acts 2:42

This pattern has repeated itself over and over throughout history. When the church is vibrant and alive, you will find the Word of God at the core of its attention and emphasis. When that fades or is set aside, you will find confusion, apathy, and a church floundering to survive a shipwreck. In order for the church to arise in the midst of a culture defined by moral relativism and secularism, there must be a revolutionary return to the simplicity of the Word of God as our source of strength. We must rediscover what we have taken for granted and fall in love all over again with the God that the Scriptures reveal to us. Mark Batterson, in his book *Primal,* states it this way:

> Reformations are *not* born out of new discoveries.
> Those are often called cults. Reformations are born out
> of rediscovering something ancient, something primal.
> They are born out of primal truths rediscovered, re-
> imagined, and radically reapplied to our lives.[6]

If we are to be sustained in the midst of a twisted and sliding society and regain our footing and stance as a prophetic voice to our culture, we must rediscover our appetite for the daily bread of God's Word. Yesterday's manna will not satisfy us. What we learned long ago will not fill us with the boldness and wisdom that we need for today's challenges. In an age where the church is caught up in looking for better methodology, what we really need is a return to the bibliocity. We need to be building our lives upon the Word of God, together, feasting on it in community. We need to be defined as the "people of the book."

DAYS OF DECEPTION

If ever there was a time when we needed to be people of the Word, it is now. While in some ways the availability of information and biblical resources should strengthen the church, it can also be argued that it has also made the church vulnerable. False teachers abound on the Internet, and alternative philosophies compete for the minds and hearts of God's people, often reinforced by the media and Hollywood. There are very few ways to effectively distinguish between false teaching and the truth. In times past churches and pastors were the gatekeepers, determining who was a wolf and who was a shepherd. Today anyone can claim to be a Bible teacher or spiritual guide and gain immediate access to anyone via the Internet.

The apostle Paul wrote to believers about the dark times that would come. He encouraged an attitude of full alert against the devil's tactics to deceive and distort.

> Now the Spirit expressly says that in the later times some will depart from the faith by devoting themselves to deceitful spirits and teachings of demons.
>
> —1 TIMOTHY 4:1

The church must be sober minded and fully aware that the devil will stop at nothing to keep the pure Word of truth out of the hearts and minds of the saints of God. The days we live in require us to "let the word of Christ dwell in us richly" (Col. 3:16) and intentionally be arrayed in the full armor of God, so that we may stand strong.

I see this played out day after day as a pastor of a local church. People have been systematically deceived by the spirit of this age into believing that something other than Jesus is the answer. Paul said that this age would be marked by traps and demonic spirits that are out to deceive people and take them captive, believing a lie. So many alternative voices are bombarding our minds that, without a strong foundation in the Word of God, we will lose our equilibrium and easily find ourselves reacting to situations and feelings instead of being anchored to the eternal, unchanging Word of God.

This seduction away from the Word has even encroached upon our pulpits and churches. The Bible has been challenged, redefined, and even banished from sermons. Pastors have become fearful to teach on certain passages of Scripture because of the fallout that may occur or the persecution we may receive. Because of a fear that we may lose market share in an ever-darkening culture, churches and movements have become more concerned about marketing than being the prophetic voice to our culture. Our crowds are enlarging, but our passion and power are dwindling.

Too many churches have reinvented the gospel of Jesus into a therapeutic, self-help set of principles that can apply to anyone in any religion as long as they have a positive attitude. If the gospel we preach from our pulpits could be preached by anyone other than a follower of Jesus, it is not the gospel. This is a diseased message that has crept in and soothed our consciences but stripped the church of the message that once upon a time turned the world upside down and prevailed against spiritual powers of darkness over cities and cultures.

> So the word of the Lord continued to increase and prevail mightily.
>
> —ACTS 19:20

The one thing that has been entrusted to the church throughout all generations is the Word of God, which was given to us as our food, our guide, and our source. We are

124

the carriers and guardians of the truth. Not only have we been commissioned to protect it, since it cannot be destroyed, but we have also been commissioned to ingest it and demonstrate its explosive power to transform. The church is meant to be the personification of the Word of God made flesh in every culture and every generation. The way we order our lives around the Word, just as the first disciples did, should demonstrate an alternative kingdom society in the midst of a world that is feeling the shifting and shaking of a world without security.

If there has ever been a time when the church must become marked by a dedication to the Word of God, it is now. Just as in other times, a reinvigorated focus and passion for the Word of God among God's people always precede a reawakening within the culture we find ourselves. We must never allow the world to affect how we interpret the Word. Instead, let the Word affect how the world interprets us. As they read our lives, let the Word prevail mightily!

BUILDING UNSHAKABLE LIVES

Ever since I was a child, I have had an unquenchable love for the Word of God. My grandparents are mostly responsible for this. Some of my earliest memories were of my sitting on their laps and them reading the Bible to me. Even before I could read it, I knew there was something special about this book. When I was twelve years old, I received a divine call to the ministry. I immediately sensed my future success would be found in building a strong foundation upon the Word of God. So I gave myself, at an early age, to intense reading and study of the Bible. King David wrote about the sustaining power of the Word of God in Psalm 119:

How can a young man keep his way pure? By guarding it according to your word. With my whole heart I seek you; let me not wander from your commandments! I have stored up your word in my heart, that I might not sin against you.

—PSALM 119:9–11

Paul wrote to Timothy, the new young pastor of the Ephesian church, about the importance and the value that Scripture should have in the life of the believer and the church as a whole.

But as for you, continue in what you have learned and have firmly believed, knowing from whom you learned and how from childhood you have been acquainted with the sacred writings, which are able to make you wise for salvation through faith in Christ Jesus. All scripture is breathed out by God and profitable for teaching, for reproof, for correction, and for training in righteousness, that the man of God may be complete, equipped for every good work.

—2 TIMOTHY 3:14–17

It is the Word of God that gives us understanding and revelation. By it we discover all that we know about God, His will, and attributes. It gives us instruction about how to be saved and fully please God. The Bible connects us and our story to the larger story of God's eternal purpose and illuminates the path of how we are to live in this world. It exposes the darkness of sin and its deceptive nature and speaks prophetically about things that are to come.

All of this comes directly from the mouth of God by revelation. Literally the words are *God-breathed* and eternal. They are immoveable and forever fixed. This is what we are called to build our lives upon in the midst of a world of darkness in which nothing is as it seems to be. There is a constant shifting and ever-changing uncertainty that paralyzes the world with fear and anxiety. The Word of God is a gift that gives us confidence and surety that God has everything under control and that His kingdom is soon to appear.

> Everyone then who hears these words of mine and does them will be like a wise man who builds his house on the rock. And the rain fell, and the floods came, and the winds blew and beat on the house, but it did not fall, because it had been founded on the rock.
>
> —MATTHEW 7:24–25

It pulls back the veil on this temporal world and gives us the perspective from the vantage point of God's kingdom. The Word of God reshapes our hearts and replaces the weak scaffolding of this world's broken system with the infrastructure of the kingdom of God. By it our minds are renewed to the will of God, enabling us to fulfill the purpose and destiny God has for our lives.

If we truly are the citizens of heaven here to colonize this world with the culture of heaven, we must become more saturated with the Word of our King and the ways of our homeland. The Bible is the spoken and transmitted decree of King Jesus, and it contains the spiritual DNA of the kingdom of God. Made up of 1,189 chapters, 66 books by more than 40 authors, the Bible is more than a book; it is our sustenance and only stability. N. T. Wright so aptly describes it this way:

> In other words, the Bible isn't there simply to be an accurate reference point for people who want to look things up and be sure they've got them right. It is there to equip God's people to carry forward his

purposes of new covenant and new creation. It is there to enable people to work for justice, to sustain their spirituality as they do so, to create and enhance relationships at every level, and to produce that new creation which will have about it something of the beauty of God himself.[7]

Chapter 7

BE SPIRIT FILLED:
IN A WORLD RUNNING ON EMPTY

If it's true that the Spirit of God dwells in us and
that our bodies are the Holy Spirit's temple, then
shouldn't there be a huge difference between the
person who has the Spirit of God living inside of him
or her and the person who does not?[1]

—FRANCIS CHAN

T'S INTERESTING TO me how often in our pursuit to
follow Jesus we are guilty of forgetting or minimizing
important elements that He seemed to place serious
emphasis upon. One of those essentials is the person of the
Holy Spirit and His empowerment. Jesus spent a significant
amount of time near the end of His ministry instructing
the disciples about this third person of the Godhead and
the necessity of His presence in fulfilling their assignment.
It was also one of the last instructions He gave them before
He ascended to the right hand of God the Father and sent
them out to carry on the mission.

You are witnesses of these things. And behold, I am
sending the promise of my Father upon you. But stay in
the city until you are clothed with power from on high.

—LUKE 24:48–49

When we read the Book of Acts, we see the fulfillment
of the coming of the Holy Spirit as Jesus promised. A group
of ragtag, uneducated Galileans were marvelously engulfed

by the deluge of the Holy Spirit and formed the church, the body of Christ. They were no longer in hiding or waiting in preparation. This was the moment of their reveal, and now they were thrust out into the open for all the world to see and hear.

This once scared and fearful band of followers were now an unstoppable force beginning in Jerusalem and spreading like a virus throughout the Roman civilization as they boldly proclaimed Jesus as the risen and exalted Messiah and true King of the world. Their message was confrontational, calling all to repent of their sins and be saved from this wicked world system. The power of the Holy Spirit had completely transformed them and empowered them supernaturally, and the world would never be the same. Miraculous signs and wonders, unusual unity, and unwavering devotion in the face of massive persecution stains all the pages of this glorious record of the first church in action.

PATTERN OR PRIORITY

One of the Bible reading habits I have developed over the years is to read through the Book of Acts about every other month or so. I have done this since Bible college days and carried it over for more than twenty years. The first time I did this intentionally, I read the entire book through in one sitting. Reading it without any break really brought the pages to life for me and challenged me to think differently. It took me less than three hours to read all twenty-eight chapters, but it has taken more than twenty years to process what I read. I asked some very important questions that day during spring break that have shaped how I view myself, the church, and the state of the church in this postmodern culture.

One of the reasons I have since determined to read it through so regularly is that I never want to lose that sense of connection and urgency that I gained the first time I read it like this. I also do it because something holy rises up within me that I cannot describe as anything other than passion to see the church that started so gloriously against all odds rediscover the person of the Holy Spirit who has in some ways been left behind as a relic of the past.

One of the questions I have asked myself over and over again, having read it literally hundreds of times, is, "What has happened to us?" What I mean by this is, "Why does the church look so differently than it did in the Book of Acts?" I am cautious in asking this question because whenever I do, I can almost predict the answers I will receive from different tribes. Some will say that the series of events recorded in the Book of Acts was a period of transition and not meant to be the norm. Others will say that Acts is a narrative, and you cannot draw accurate theology from reading a narrative. (Tell that to the writers of the Gospels!) Some who come from a more Pentecostal perspective would like to repeat the Book of Acts in every detail.

While I don't believe that the answer for the church living in the twenty-first century is to necessarily emulate everything that we find in the Book of Acts (there are a lot of things that the apostles would encourage us not to repeat, because they weren't good the first time they happened), I do believe the core idea of this most famous sequel is "the church empowered." This must be our takeaway and our return destination.

One of the values that we have had from the very beginning of Radiant Church is to be unapologetic of the priority we place upon the Holy Spirit's presence and prominence in all we do. But also we don't want to allow the Holy Spirit to be sensationalized by "super-spirituals" who have a personal agenda to "use" Him for entertainment instead of "entertaining" Him and being willing to be used by Him as He wills.

We refer to our position as "contending for the radical middle," and it is a very difficult position to hold to because on each side of the road of truth there is a ditch of error and ignorance that we could easily fall into. We don't hold the position of "contending for the radical middle" because we are watering down or putting a seatbelt on the Holy Spirit, but we realize the heart and the purpose for the Holy Spirit and make sure they aren't hijacked.

Our heart is to be authentic in our awareness and undiluted in our expression of the power and presence. We want all that God wants and nothing He doesn't. We want the authentic and undiluted power and demonstration of the Holy Spirit and have come to realize that nothing less will empower us to clearly demonstrate the kingdom of God as a present reality.

As a result of constantly self-evaluating and going back to our original desire to be a church that is "empowered for mission," as we see in the Book of Acts, we have also come to some conclusions about what is and isn't a priority for us as a church and what it means to be "Spirit-filled" in a world running on empty. Those conclusions are what will follow in this chapter.

Open Arms and Open Hearts

Much of the church is confused about the Holy Spirit. Arguments have raged for as long as the church has existed about how to handle this "God in third person." Part of the problem is that the Holy Spirit is not meant to be "handled" or controlled and is not necessarily predictable. He is also the most mysterious person within the Godhead. Most of us have a context for understanding God as Father. Whether we have had a good and loving father relationship in our lives or not, we can at least draw upon examples to form an internal understanding of what it means.

Jesus, the second person of the Trinity, came as Immanuel, God with us. The Incarnation was and is one of the most mysterious and glorious events to ever take place within human history. This and the Resurrection are the two miracles upon which the Christian faith is built. While we don't understand the "how" of it, we do gain the "who" of it. Jesus revealed who and how God is. Even though we weren't there to walk with Him as the first disciples did, we read the words of the witnesses found in the Gospels, and we discover who Jesus was and what He was about. We can relate to His humanity and stand in awe of His divinity.

The Holy Spirit is a different matter altogether. There is no frame of reference for us to grasp this invisible God or comprehend His mode of operation. Jesus compared Him to the wind, totally unpredictable and mysterious (John 3:8). Because of this some are tempted to relegate Him to being a "force" instead of a person. Some Christians acknowledge the existence of the Holy Spirit doctrinally yet in practice live out their faith as partial agnostics, ignoring one-third of the Godhead.

The Holy Spirit is very much a person, and because He is a person, He desires relationship. He has emotions and can either be grieved or welcomed. Consider the following verses:

> And do not grieve the Holy Spirit of God, by whom you were sealed for the day of redemption.
>
> —EPHESIANS 4:30

> May the grace of the Lord Jesus Christ, the love of God, and the fellowship of the Holy Spirit be with you all.
>
> —2 CORINTHIANS 13:14, NLT

He is with us on assignment and given to us for more than a token. He is given to empower, lead, and counsel us individually and the church corporately. While He is always present in the life of every believer, He is not always acknowledged. That is our responsibility. We decide whether we will open our hearts to hear His voice and follow His leading or keep Him in the background.

> Spell this out in capital letters: THE HOLY SPIRIT IS A PERSON. He is not enthusiasm. He is not courage. He is not energy. He is not the personification of all good qualities, like Jack Frost is the personification of cold weather. Actually, the Holy Spirit is not the personification of anything. He is a Person, the same as you are a person, but not material substance. He has individuality. He is one being and not another. He has will and intelligence. He has hearing. He has knowledge and sympathy and ability to love and see and think. He can hear, speak, desire, grieve and rejoice. He is a Person.[2]
>
> —A. W. Tozer

For the church to effectively engage culture and demonstrate the glory of God to our generation, we desperately need a renewed sense of hunger and dependency upon the Holy Spirit. We must open up our hearts intentionally and welcome and invite the Holy Spirit to come and take the lead in our lives and churches.

Nothing can replace what God intended to lead, fill, and empower His vehicle of kingdom extension—the church. We can fill up on the temporal things of this world, but they will not fuel us to live to our fullest potential. The engine of the church was meant to burn with power from the heavenly oil alone. To fill us with anything less would be like filling up our cars and trucks with water and expecting them to perform correctly.

The head of the church is Jesus, but the leader and foreman

of the church on the earth is the Holy Spirit. To tune Him out or leave Him on the shelf as something that is optional for us because we are "uncomfortable" with what we cannot control or see is the greatest mistake we could make. Without a renewed sense of open arms to the Holy Spirit, there is no possibility that the church can possibly navigate the waters of a world in turmoil. We will live no different than the world we are trying to illuminate. We will live limited by worldly intellect, principles, and methods, all of which will not impress anyone. We will remain indistinguishable, and the flame of our lamp will continue to dim. We cannot afford any longer to run on empty.

Why would we choose to live out our faith with our arms tightly folded, refusing to embrace the partner that God saw fit to give us? Why would we close our minds and hearts off to the supernatural influence of the Helper in exchange for the logic of man? It all begins by recognizing that right now He is here and ready to lead, ready to empower, ready to light up our lives, if we only acknowledge and pursue Him beyond the safety zone of normal.

Sent to Lead the Way

Jesus prepared the disciples for the ministry thrust that was out before them. He told them that it was to their advantage that He was leaving them because now He was going to send what He described as "another helper." I am sure to the disciples this sounded like crazy talk. "How in the world could it be better than having Jesus right here with us?" I bet if you took a poll of Christians today and asked them, "Would you rather be living during the time that Jesus ministered on the earth in person or would you rather live now, as a believer filled with the Spirit?" the majority would automatically choose the former. But this isn't what Jesus emphasized to them, and the same goes for us today.

I did not say these things to you from the beginning, because I was with you. But now I am going to him who sent me, and none of you asks me, "Where are you going?" But because I have said these things to you, sorrow has filled your heart. Nevertheless, I tell you the truth; it is to your advantage that I go away, for if I do not go away, the Helper will not come to you. But if I go, I will send him to you.

—JOHN 16:4–7

This word for *helper* is the Greek word *parakletos* and can be translated as "advocate, encourager, counselor, aid or legal advisor." Jesus said the Holy Spirit would come as "another helper," meaning, equal with Himself. He would come to help and assist us in walking out the purpose that God has for us. This is different from walking with Jesus in person (and more beneficial to us) because this "Helper" or *paraklete* would not lead from the outside in a fixed geographical location but indwelling each of us, regardless of time, space, or age.

Jesus described the Holy Spirit's presence as something unique to His followers. While we are living in the midst of this world in the present, broken age, we are now becoming the recipients of the Spirit of God, something this world is incapable of receiving.

And I will ask the Father, and he will give you another Helper, to be with you forever, even the Spirit of truth, whom the world cannot receive, because it neither sees him nor knows him. You know him, for he dwells with you and will be in you.

—JOHN 14:16–17

This is an interesting statement to ponder. We have something from God that the world cannot receive, imitate, or manipulate. We have this treasure from heaven: God's supernatural indwelling, meant to divinely lead us and assist us as we live in this world. The Holy Spirit, who hovered over the face of a darkened planet filled with chaos and void in the very beginning, is once again creating. He is shaping our hearts to be new creations in Christ Jesus through the work of sanctification, and He is working in this evil-influenced age of darkness by indwelling and leading the church as we demonstrate the kingdom of God supernaturally. This is new creation work, and it is to what we have been called. We do not accomplish this with the tools of this world, because all that would be built is Babel, which is symbolic of man's ingenuity independent of God. We build by the leading and the empowerment of the Holy Spirit, who is the giver of the "power of the age to come."

> ...who have tasted the heavenly gift, and have shared
> in the Holy Spirit, and have tasted the goodness of
> the word of God and the powers of the age to come...
>
> —HEBREWS 6:4–5

When we closely examine the ministry of Jesus, it is hard to escape or write off the significance of the role the Holy Spirit played. From the very beginning of His ministry we see His actions were constantly led and directed by the Spirit. He was anointed by the Holy Spirit, and He was led by the Holy Spirit in all that He did.

> ...how God anointed Jesus of Nazareth with the Holy
> Spirit and with power. He went about doing good and
> healing all who were oppressed by the devil, for God
> was with him.
>
> —ACTS 10:38

Then Jesus was led up by the Spirit into the wilderness to be tempted by the devil.

—Matthew 4:1

When you think about the adversity Jesus faced from the religious leaders, political leaders, and demands of the crowds, it is amazingly supernatural to consider all that He did within three and a half short years. He was able to do this because He remained in constant communion with the Father and the Holy Spirit.

The disciples learned this firsthand as they were mentored under Jesus's ministry style and way of life. They repeated the same pattern that they saw in Jesus, receiving the Holy Spirit in power before beginning any ministry endeavors. They had experienced what it was like to minister out of their own intellect and know-how. As we read about the explosive growth of the church from Pentecost on, it becomes extremely obvious that they had left that mentality behind and traded it for a complete dependence and developed sensitivity to the Holy Spirit's direction and leading. In almost every decision, every persecution, in every open door and opportunity, they sought for direction. As they preached, the Holy Spirit gave them the words to say. There was not a part of the early church's expansion or development that was unaffected by the Holy Spirit. Even one of the most uncomfortable passages of Scripture in the entire New Testament, where Ananias and Sapphira conspired to lie about their offering and were killed by God (that should test some of our theology right there!), is an example to us of how the Holy Spirit was leading the way.

What about us? Have things changed so drastically that we no longer need to be led in the same way? What has changed? Of course we are far more technologically advanced than they were in the first century. Science has made huge breakthroughs; medicine has radically reduced disease and epidemics. We can now travel anywhere in the world in less than twenty-four hours, and we can instantly communicate with people all over the world. Maybe we don't need the Holy Spirit as "they" needed Him. Maybe we have enough information available through the Internet and education that the kind of supernatural direction and miraculous intervention is no longer needed. Perhaps we have outgrown the Holy Spirit.

Or perhaps we have been deceived into believing a lie that has also stripped us of our birthright and domesticated the church. Think about all that the church was able to do in the first century without the printing press, mass communication, freedom of speech, easy travel, democracy, or the Internet. There was no Facebook or Twitter to spread the word. They systematically overthrew the most powerful pagan empire the world had ever seen and sparked a movement of righteousness throughout the earth that today claims almost one-third of the world's population. In the face of martyrdom, threat of heresy, and constant demonic attack the church thrived as it was led and empowered by the Holy Spirit.

What *could* the church of Acts have done with all of the tools you and I have at our disposal combined with what they knew of the power and the presence of the anointing? Of course that will never be known because they didn't have it. But what about us? We do have it, and the potential is there for the church with its best efforts and opportunities to regain and rediscover the abiding Helper who is ready to lead us into uncharted waters.

Being people who are finding our leadership in the person of the Holy Spirit is not optional but mandatory. It is the only way forward for anyone who desires to cut through the darkness of this age. Paul commanded the Galatians to continue to walk in step with the direction of the Holy Spirit.

> Since we are living by the Spirit, let us follow the Spirit's leading *in every part of our lives.*
> —Galatians 5:25, nlt, emphasis added

We have a choice to make. Will we attempt to live out our purpose in our own strength or take Jesus up on His invitation to a deeper fellowship with the Holy Spirit? Will we attempt to know the Jesus we love and serve through the lens of history and secondhand experience or tune our hearts in to hear the voice of the Holy Spirit who Jesus said would "bear witness of Him"? He wants to lead us into all truth, but first we must lay aside the lie—the lie that we don't need Him any longer or the lie that He is no longer available to us.

As a pastor I can tell you that there is no way "in this world" that I could possibly lead a growing church of thousands of people without the leading of the Holy Spirit. Daily my time of prayer and worship is the single most important appointment I have. I have learned to listen to the promptings and the impressions I sense during these times, knowing that it is my Helper who is leading the way. I have had to make so many pivotal decisions over the years that have affected the entire direction of our ministry. I can honestly say that the decisions I made out of insecurity or fear have been the worst decisions of my life. But when I listen and obey the voice of the God, grace always abounds, and we have seen God show up in huge, supernatural ways. I have determined that I don't want to lead the church anywhere that the Holy Spirit is not directing.

I don't believe that the leadership assignment of the Holy Spirit is reserved for just those who are in the fivefold ministry offices. There are not two classes of Christians: those whom God speaks to directly and then those who need a moderator. God is willing and able to speak to each of us and lead us into all the truth we need at any given moment. Every Christian is indwelt by the same Holy Spirit and is called to live a dynamic, supernatural life marked by God-given direction and guidance. But we are responsible for welcoming His counsel and developing a listening ear so that we keep in step with the work He wants to accomplish in us and then through us.

What we call supernatural should be natural to a believer. It shouldn't be considered "super-normal" as if it were the exception. The defining mark of the children of God is that they will be "led by the Spirit of God" (Rom. 8:14). The Holy Spirit will lead us in so many ways if we learn to trust and listen. What we can be confident of is that He has our best interests in mind and always leads us into a closer, more intimate relationship with the Father. He is our constant reminder that we are not alone and we have not been abandoned. He reveals Jesus to us and connects our hearts to the Father-heart of God that then motivates us to please and love Him and to believe with full trust and assurance that God is directing our steps toward a destination. He constantly reminds us that we are not orphans. We are part of the kingdom of God and part of the royal family. Regardless of what label this world tries to plaster on us to shape us or affect the trajectory of our lives and decisions, our boldness and confidence come from knowing that the Helper has been sent and is with us now.

LIVING IN HOT PURSUIT

The first Bible college I attended was a traditional, evangelical school that had a strong emphasis upon solid biblical interpretation, which included a cessationist view relating to the gifts and ministry of the Holy Spirit. Cessationists believe that the supernatural and miraculous gifts and demonstrations of the Spirit have now passed and those gifts such as tongues, prophecy, and healing have now passed. At first when I registered to go to school there, I thought that this wasn't such a big deal. After all, we agreed on so much relating to the basics of doctrine that we should be able to move beyond this minor disagreement.

I came to love so many of my professors and was truly inspired by so many of the students and faculty and their love for God and passion for missions. There were so many things I learned about grace and biblical studies that stand out to me from that time. I am truly grateful for the time I spent there—which, by the way, wasn't very long.

I soon discovered that this "minor" disagreement wasn't so minor to some people. I found myself as one of just a few charismatic students in the entire student body. Class after class became a debate and conversation that became very combative and accusatory toward me and the ideas I stood for. To believe that God still spoke, still healed, and used average people to do it was a complete offense to them and their logic. I was told that it either had to be demonic or delusion if I believed that the Holy Spirit was still doing "the stuff," as John Wimber used to call it.

This was one of the most difficult and yet most pivotal seasons in my life and preparation. Not only did I have a heavy class load, but I also found myself having to deconstruct everything I had ever been taught about the Holy Spirit. I had to be able to explain the theological perspective on every paper and test and reexamine why I believed what I did at the same time. I compare that season to tearing down a car, piece by piece, and then rebuilding it to completion.

The result was that after just a year and a half, a decision was made that I would not pursue a theological degree from this institution and we would part ways. My counselor told me that they had realized they were not going to change my views and that I obviously wasn't going to change theirs. We were at a stalemate. I needed to "pursue my studies elsewhere" was the conclusion. I had put a stake in the ground and decided that the Holy Spirit's presence and power in my life were a pursuit worth fighting for. Instead of pursuing this particular degree, I was going to live my life in pursuit of something more valuable and powerful to the ministry that God had for me than any class I opted out of. I wanted the power of the Holy Spirit.

I remember reading an article one time about what has been referred to as the "Jeffersonian Bible." It was a Bible that Thomas Jefferson, one of the Founding Fathers of the American Revolution, had created by going through the New Testament and cutting out all of the verses that referred to anything miraculous or supernatural. All references to healing, miracles, and the Resurrection itself were removed so that what was left was what Jefferson believed revealed the true, original ethic and the divine morality taught by Jesus. He believed this was the true form of Christianity.

Unfortunately there are many today who have, to a lesser degree, done a similar thing to the Scriptures. While not necessarily going to this extreme, when we dismiss the supernatural aspects of God's working with humanity, we are left with very little in the New Testament (and the Old Testament for that matter) that is applicable for us today. It's almost as if we have two faiths and two worlds.

Paul was the greatest church planter and missionary the world has ever known. He took the gospel that originally was limited to a Jewish context and introduced it to new frontiers in the Gentile world. He contextualized the gospel and was responsible for the rapid advance of the gospel throughout Asia Minor and Europe. Paul planted more churches and developed more Gentile leaders than any of the other apostles. When Paul entered a new city or culture, he honored his Jewish heritage by bringing the gospel to the synagogues first. When he preached to the Greeks, who were intellectuals and the caretakers of generations of philosophical wisdom, Paul refused to diminish the gospel to wisdom alone but engaged in supernatural demonstration of the presence and validity of the kingdom of God. He did not just appeal to their minds, but he also brought the power of the Holy Spirit to bear.

> And I, when I came to you, brothers, did not come proclaiming to you the testimony of God with lofty speech or wisdom. For I decided to know nothing among you except Jesus Christ and him crucified. And I was with you in weakness and in fear and much trembling, and my speech and my message were not in plausible words of wisdom, but in demonstration of the Spirit and of power, so that your faith might not rest in the wisdom of men but in the power of God.
>
> —1 CORINTHIANS 2:1–5

The result was a thriving church full of new converts. Over the course of time this church began to experience several significant problems. Key members were living in rabid immorality, schisms were forming around various leaders and teachers, and there were massive excesses taking place in regard to spiritual gifts. These problems became so dominant that Paul dedicated an entire letter to address the situations. First Corinthians not only answered the leadership's concerns, but it has also become a template epistle for the church to draw from over the years for how to approach the supernatural elements of the Holy Spirit within a pagan, dysfunctional, and intellectually dominant culture.

> Now concerning spiritual gifts, brothers, I do not
> want you to be uninformed.
>
> —1 CORINTHIANS 12:1

> Now there are varieties of gifts, but the same spirit;
> and there are varieties of service, but the same Lord;
> and there are varieties of activities, but it is the same
> God who empowers them all in everyone. To each is
> given the manifestation of the Spirit for the common
> good. For to one is given through the Spirit the utter-
> ance of wisdom, and to another the utterance of knowl-
> edge according to the same Spirit, to another faith by
> the same Spirit, to another gifts of healing by the one
> Spirit, to another the working of miracles, to another
> prophecy, to another the ability to distinguish between
> spirits, to another various kinds of tongues, to another
> the interpretation of tongues. All these are empowered
> by one and the same Spirit, who apportions to each
> one individually as he wills.
>
> —1 CORINTHIANS 12:4–11

In reading these words of Paul, I can't find anything
that remotely resembles an attitude that communicates that
the manifestation of the Holy Spirit in miraculous ways is
a "take it or leave it" proposition. In fact, he says that he
does not want believers to be ignorant. Ignorance can come
as a result of not knowing or as a result of intentionally
"ignoring" something we are uncomfortable with.

Some have chosen to ignore or avoid discussion and pursuit of the gifts because of their controversial nature or due
to some excesses they have seen or heard over the years.
Still others are just simply unaware that God still desires
for His church to be filled with believers who are filled with
His presence and overflowing with signs that His kingdom
is come. There is fear in some that we will run people off

from our churches if we are too "spiritual," and so we adjust to make it palatable. But in our pursuit of acceptance are we losing something at a very high cost? Pastor Jack Hayford writes in his book *Living the Spirit-Formed Life:*

> But God isn't impressed by either intellectual or emotional sophistry. And as for society, it's a question of degree: How far will you go to please the world? We may feel we must pamper worldly-mindedness by cooling our praise in church. But inevitably, the flesh will prompt us to cool our message, our convictions and our lifestyle as Christians. So before you dampen your praise or demonstrative worship or witnessing, consider just how much "cool" you think will ultimately satisfy the world.[3]

Whatever the reason, whether abuse or avoidance, Paul makes it clear that a faith that is solely constructed by an intellectual approach and logical reasoning is not a faith that will stand, regardless of the age we are living in.

He unashamedly encourages every believer to be motivated by love and to strongly desire spiritual gifts—to pursue them, not pacify them. We need more than just the idea of the Holy Spirit's presence in our lives; we need tangible aid of heaven's helper flowing through our lives in supernatural ways. We must be continually filled with the Holy Spirit in a world that drains us of our heavenly reality day after day. The Holy Spirit is the presence of the kingdom of God within us and the guarantee of what is still to come. He brings with Him the genetic code of God's nature revealed through us in the fruit that we bear (Gal. 5:22) when our hearts are fully captivated and surrendered to Him. He also comes with power, completely saturating our being with His presence and "dynamic" power for ministry.

The apostles knew their dependency upon the Holy Spirit.

Why is the church so quick to assume that we can make any significant difference or live up to our call without the supernatural touch from the Holy Spirit? How can we love the way Jesus loved without the Holy Spirit's help? How can we treat God's gifts to us as a salad bar, where we choose which ingredients we want and those that we don't? We desperately need it all. What would it look like if every believer in every church fully embraced the Holy Spirit as the leader and empowerer of our lives? What if all of those parts of Jefferson's Bible that were removed were highlighted and circled in our Bibles as the focus of our pursuit?

RUNNING ON EMPTY

I have a tendency to run my car down to where it's almost beyond the empty mark. Oftentimes I wait long after the "ding" goes off and the light flashes on the dashboard before I actually stop to refuel. Most of the time I am aware of how low I have allowed the gas gauge to get, but I procrastinate anyway. A few times this has resulted in me being stuck on the side of the road, unable to go anywhere and in need of someone to bail me out with a gas can and a smile. You would think I would learn my lesson and never let it get down that low again, but unfortunately I do.

The church has a tendency to run dangerously low on the Holy Spirit. I am not making a theological statement as much as an experiential statement. The world around us is constantly on the verge of an impending energy crisis. The volatility in the price of a barrel of oil skyrockets and then plunges, sending economies into free falls and creating panic in people's hearts. Lines at gas stations extend out into the streets when a rumor of a disturbance in the overseas market hits the news wires.

These energy concerns should be dwarfed by the urgency we should feel upon realizing how much we are attempting to do in our own strength. Eventually our strength will either come to nothing or become exhausted. In either case human power or ability can never replace the demonstration of heavenly power that declares the presence of the kingdom in our midst.

What we see in the natural reflects a deeper spiritual reality. Our world is running on empty in more ways than one. But the church should not be in this place. Our inheritance is not lack or shortage but overflow and abundance. When there is an oil shortage in the lamp stand of the church, it is due our neglect and not God's design.

Jesus didn't send us the Holy Spirit as a "once filled, always filled" gift. We must be continually filled, over and over again, a steady stream of heavenly energy and intimacy from the resources of heaven. We need to carefully monitor the dashboards of our lives and our churches to see where we are. As you go through the Book of Acts, one pattern prevails: the church was filled with the Holy Spirit often. To do otherwise will leave us on the side of the road holding our Bibles close but with little power or passion left to make any further progress. Our boldness will wane, and our vision will become blurry. When we come to realize as the first Christians did that the Holy Spirit is ready to move from being a trickle in our lives to becoming a mighty overflowing river from our lives, we will discover that we never have to redline it ever again. He is the Helper and Empowerer sent to fill the church with the glorious presence of Jesus.

Chapter 8

BE PEOPLE ORIENTED:
IN A SELF-CENTERED SOCIETY

> Being unwanted, unloved, uncared for, forgotten by
> everybody, I think that is a much greater hunger,
> a much greater poverty than the person who has
> nothing to eat.[1]
>
> —MOTHER TERESA

LAST YEAR JANE and I had an opportunity to go on a pilgrimage to Israel. It had always been a lifelong dream of mine, and our church, knowing this, surprised us after fifteen years of pastoring by sending us for an almost two-week trip. I was ecstatic! The night before our trip I could not sleep thinking about all the places we were going to see. I recounted in my mind all of the biblical stories and their locations and consulted our tour schedule to see when and where we would be visiting what.

The next morning, very early, we set off on this adventure. We drove to Chicago and boarded the airplane for the very long transatlantic flight. Once again I found it difficult to sleep because my mind was already walking the landscape of the Holy Land, where Jesus and the patriarchs walked. Finally we arrived in Tel Aviv, and my feet touched the ground in Israel for the first time. It was an awesome experience to walk outside of the airport and look all around me and realize *this was where it all happened.*

Over the next several days we traveled the length and the breadth of Israel (which was surprisingly smaller than I had imagined). We stayed in a hotel next to the Sea of

Galilee, climbed our way up to the fortress of Masada, and entered the city of Jerusalem, quoting the Psalms of Ascent as we went. We walked the Temple Mount and prayed at the Western Wall where Jews have prayed for centuries. Perhaps most powerful of all the experiences we had was visiting Golgotha and the Garden Tomb where it is believed that Jesus died and then rose again from the dead.

We stood in line waiting for our turn to enter this ancient tomb. The anticipation was huge as we literally stood upon the ground just feet from where the Son of God was resurrected and the stone was rolled away by angels that first Easter morning. When we finally entered the tomb, we went in just a few at a time. It is not very large at all inside, and the slab of limestone upon which Jesus's body would have been laid was gated off from the standing area we were in, keeping us looking at it from a distance through the metal bars. Just then a couple, led by a different tour guide entered, being led carefully by the hand over the threshold. These two were pilgrims from Europe who also happened to be blind. The tour guide unlocked the gate that separated the area we were in from the place where Jesus's body had been laid and allowed them to walk through the restricted area to the stone outcropping and touch it with their hands. Even though they were unable to see the tomb, their other senses were engaged as they felt this sacred space. As I watched this happen just feet away, standing in the tomb, the Holy Spirit spoke to me and said, "Everyone comes to this place blind, but blessed is he who leaves seeing." I was stunned by this event and continued to think about it long after we stepped out of the tomb back into the garden area with the rest of our tour group.

Over the last couple days of being in Israel, at every stop we made I prayed a silent prayer that basically said, "God, give me eyes to see what You want me to see here." I have to admit that I really didn't get much more than the one statement He had already given me until we were back in the airport about to leave for home.

As I was waiting in the lobby for our plane to board, I was contemplating what that message had really meant and if I had really grasped what God was trying to say to me. Of course I knew the obvious application was that the power of the Resurrection has opened our eyes to new life in Jesus. I remembered the words of Jesus to Simon Peter when He told him that flesh and blood had not revealed who He was, but the Father who is in heaven. But I knew that there was more that God was trying to say to me. Then, very tenderly, the Holy Spirit spoke to me again, "Lee, each of these places that you have visited here are just dirt, rock, and water—relics of the past. They have no significance beyond the stories they are attached to in your Bible. The reason they have meaning has nothing to do with their beauty or location. It has everything to do with the people and their stories that are connected to them. These places are important because they mark a time and place in which God did something extraordinary to intervene in the lives of people. God loves people, and so you must as well."

Ultimately the takeaway that all of us as followers of Jesus need to have is that *people are what the story of salvation is all about. The rest is only staging and decor.*

A Disconnected World

Have you ever stood in a large sea of people and felt all alone? It's possible to physically be surrounded by thousands of people but practically be disconnected and feel alone. The difference is relationship—how we see people and the value we place on them over other external and internal factors. It's amazing to me that we have more people alive at the same time on Planet Earth right now than all the people who have ever lived combined! And yet we are a very lonely, disconnected generation made up of isolated individuals. We have more tools for travel and communication, but ironically we are more isolated and segmented than ever before.

We live virtual lives that have virtually no time for or interest in what is going on in our immediate space. We can travel anywhere in the world in under twenty-four hours, and yet we don't know the neighbors who live across the street. We commute to and from work, pull into our garages, and electronically close the world out behind us. Our interaction with the world takes place on digitized screens, always on our own terms. We talk on our mobile phones to people on the other side of the planet as we pass by the people who live and work in our own community. We are connected to everything, but we belong to virtually nothing. This is the story of our postmodern society.

It is in the midst of this self-absorbed, hyper-paced society that the church is called to shine brightly as the light of the world. I believe that the church is the community of the kingdom of God, called to demonstrate to the world what the culture of heaven is really like and what God is really like. The church is called the "household" and "family" of God throughout the New Testament because this is a reality God wants us to both experience and express.

This "kingdom community" has more to offer the world than perhaps has previously been obvious at first glance. At the core of the human experience is the pursuit of belonging to something that is real, relational, and revolutionary, something that brings context for our lives and experiences and helps us find our tribe.

In all of our technological advances what we have lost is a sense of community centered around purpose. This is the essence of the word *fellowship* in the Scriptures. Fellowship is not just the idea of attending something on a certain day but the idea of dynamically belonging to something bigger than ourselves—a unity and *togetherness* that is derived from a common experience and cause, a place where we are more than a set of seven digits or a face on a social networking site. Everyone wants to be noticed, valued, and seen as significant. Everyone wants to know that their story is heard, that others know they exist. At the center of our problem with loneliness is the pursuit of belonging. We are looking for a family, a tribe to belong to, and a cause we can pour our lives into. The good news that lies at the center of the gospel is God is seeking the very same thing. He was pursuing us long before we ever considered Him or His agenda.

The idea of God's complete sufficiency within Himself is a theological construct central to a whole, biblical understanding of the nature of God as "holy." But a deeper inspection into this concept of holiness reveals that even within God's person and nature, community and relationship are also central. God dwells eternally in "Trinity"—Father, Son and Holy Spirit, a divine community. God must dwell within community because without relationship within Himself, there is no way for God to express fully who He is, which is love. Love requires others.

There has never been a time when God has been alone because there has never been a time when God was anything other than perfect love. It is out of this perfect, eternal relationship and love within the Godhead that God decided to create. All of creation flows from God's perfect desire to express fully His divine attributes and create an environment to stage the ultimate revelation of who He truly is and to be glorified within it. Mankind was made by God, in the likeness of God, in order to understand and relate to this revelation of God and ultimately be His people, His family, and His reward; to love God and experience His love and grace firsthand; and to enjoy eternally all that He has created as our inheritance. Loneliness is the by-product of our independence. It has no place within the plan of God or the desire of God. Separation was never God's intent, but it is the consequence of our rejection.

THE CROSSROADS OF BELONGING

The greatest expression of God's love for us was the sending of His Son, Jesus, in the act of the Incarnation. He willingly affected the state of fellowship within the Trinity in order to pursue the lost race of humanity. This miraculous coming of God as *one of us* in order to reconcile *all of us* is one of the two pillars that our Christian faith is built upon (the other being the resurrection of Christ) and still silences the greatest egos among us. Jesus came, revealing the will of the Father, to break the chains of bondage to sin, open our eyes to who God really is, and release us from the solitary confinement of our un-belonging. Everything Jesus taught and demonstrated was leading somewhere—to the cross.

It has been said that "X marks the spot." In the case of the cross of Christ, it is a true statement that the X marks the spot within history where God violently broke down every barrier and buffer that had ever separated us from Him. With every blow to the body of Jesus and every drop of blood that fell from His veins, God was absorbing our isolation and rejection, removing our shame and sentence of death. With His arms spread out wide, suspended between heaven and earth, this Savior was both bearing our sins and welcoming the world back into the arms of God.

Jesus became the mediator between God and man and the lover of our souls, making our return home possible. Forgiveness wasn't a concession that God begrudgingly made; it was the intent all along in order for God to receive what

He had always wanted—a family of redeemed ones who willingly worship Him. He sacrificed and moved people from the brokenness of self-centric striving to the wholeness of God-centered living.

> Christ brought us together through his death on the cross. The Cross got us to embrace, and that was the end of the hostility. Christ came and preached peace to you outsiders and peace to us insiders. He treated us as equals, and so made us equals. Through him we both share the same Spirit and have equal access to the Father.
>
> That's plain enough, isn't it? You're no longer wandering exiles. This kingdom of faith is now your home country. You're no longer strangers or outsiders. You belong here, with as much right to the name Christian as anyone. God is building a home. He's using us all—irrespective of how we got here—in what he is building. He used the apostles and prophets for the foundation. Now he's using you, fitting you in brick by brick, stone by stone, with Christ Jesus as the cornerstone that holds all the parts together. We see it taking shape day after day—a holy temple built by God, all of us built into it, a temple in which God is quite at home.
>
> —EPHESIANS 2:16–22, THE MESSAGE

God as a master architect has been hard at work building something. Jesus told the disciples early on that He would build His church—a house, a family made up of misfits and exiles. It's a shame that too often the church is more known for what and who we stand against and as an institution of exclusion. David Kinnaman, in his informative book *Unchristian: What A New Generation Really Thinks About Christianity... and Why It Matters*, states it this way:

Currently Christianity is known for being *unlike* Jesus; one of the best ways to shift that perception would be to esteem and serve outsiders. This means being compassionate, soft-hearted, and kind to people who are different from us, even hostile toward us.... Our future reputation as Christians is intricately connected to our passion for justice, service, and sacrifice.[2]

While the cross meant momentary separation of the Father from the Son, His willingness to turn His face from Jesus meant the bringing in of us who had previously been outsiders. This is the story of the church. It is to be the community of the redeemed, held together by the mortar of our stories, fashioned and placed side by side, and raised up as a beacon of God's selfless and sacrificial love in the midst of a world obsessed with self-image, self-improvement, and self-aggrandizing. The church is the ongoing witness of selfless beauty and the shocking wonder of the cross. It's meant to be a place that screams to the world, "You belong here!"

A TALE OF TWO CHURCHES

When Jane and I were first married, we found ourselves in the place of "church shopping." I hate that term, but it oftentimes fits the feeling that comes with trying to answer the question of where we belong. We had been a part of a church plant in the inner city even before we were married, but after a couple months of serving there, it became apparent that it wasn't the ideal place for us. We decided it was important for us to start our marriage upon a strong foundation, which would include a church family that we could both grow in.

We had been given several invitations from friends to come visit their churches and references to others that had good reputations. Our church backgrounds were very different from each other's. I had grown up Pentecostal, and

Jane had grown up Christian Reformed, so finding the right church was going to be an interesting experience. After a couple weeks we narrowed it down to two churches left that we felt we really needed to attend. Both of them had come highly recommended, and both of them were nondenominational and embraced the power of the Holy Spirit as well as sound biblical doctrine.

Our visit to the first church took place on a Sunday evening. We pulled into the parking lot with some pretty high expectations. We had heard that this particular church was really growing and full of young couples like us. We really hoped that we would connect well and find a home to belong to.

To say that our experience was disappointing would be an understatement. From the very first moment we got out of our car we felt like outsiders (and we were). We walked toward the building from the middle of the parking lot, alongside several other couples who were arriving at the same time. Several of them began to greet each other as they walked, but no one even made eye contact with us. When we finally made it to the front doors, I thought for sure greeters or someone would say something, but to my surprise, the guy entering in front of us didn't even hold the door open for us. We walked in past the greeters, past the crowds, and into the main sanctuary doors to find a seat. Still no eye contact, no greeting. We were invisible.

We found a seat about ten rows from the front sitting near the aisle. We were about fifteen minutes early so we sat and waited for the service to begin. We watched the worship team practice and noticed several ushers walk by us with not even so much as a hello. We were two of only a dozen or so people in the room, but it was as if we did not even exist. I felt as if we were in the Twilight Zone. A few moments later the worship leader walked off the stage, directly at us and right on by us. I turned to Jane and said, "I bet we could get up and walk out of this place without anyone even saying anything to us." She responded, "Let's try!"

We were able to walk back out of the sanctuary, past the ushers, past the crowds, past the greeters, through the doors, and to our car without a syllable being spoken or an eye catching ours. We were absolutely blown away.

Thankfully the other church that we had on our list was just down the street and also had a Sunday evening service. (Most churches back in the day had Sunday evening services.) By the time we arrived at the next church, our expectations were significantly lower than they had been a bit earlier. We entered the lobby and were immediately welcomed and invited to find a seat. When the praise and worship was done, the pastor encouraged everyone to turn and greet one another. This great couple immediately turned to Jane and me and introduced themselves. They noticed that we were new and made us feel so special. They went out of their way after the service to invite us to attend the small group that met in their home and told us that if we needed anything at all, to just look for them. This kind couple made quite an impression upon us. They were obviously well-established people within this church and had no shortage of friends and acquaintances. They didn't need our friendship. But this particular day, maybe even unknown to them, they helped a young couple feel connected. We needed to find a place to fit, and they were the reason we stuck. Resurrection Life became our home church and eventually would also become our sending church as young church planters launching out to pioneer a new kingdom community that would become known as Radiant Church.

I have often thought about what would've happened had the circumstances been different. What would've happened had we felt welcome at the other church? What if we had had a similar experience at the latter church as the former? What I do know for sure is that our experiences that day became pivotal in how we would view the church and the importance we would place upon creating a culture of belonging.

IRRESISTIBLE GRACE

The fact that we live in a self-centered world that tends to overlook, underestimate, and leave behind is an opportunity for the church to step up and lead differently. Seth Godin speaks of this opportunity as finding the "discomfort" within society and meeting the felt need.[3] It's in the void of this discomfort that the pain of exclusion and isolation is magnified, and it's in this vacuum that the church can thrive and shine most brightly if only we will see through the eyes of the cross itself. When the church resists the self-centered value system of this corrupt culture, we will become irresistible to a generation that is desperately searching and starving for a place to call home.

In a world that labels and judges everything within a nanosecond, the cross offers the gift of life-transforming grace that can overcome those judgments—the hope to become what we were always meant to be and the grace that brings forgiveness and the invitation to a new beginning. This is the message of the cross.

God didn't just have a view *of* the cross, but He also had a view *from* the cross. While you and I look to the cross and are left speechless at the undeserved death of Jesus that brought about our undeserved ransom, God is also viewing us from the vantage point of the one suffering in the name of love. Instead of condemning us with the labels and judgments that we so rightfully deserve and the world is so ready to post over our heads as our true identity, Jesus looked out across the spectrum of our shame and sin and offered us ridiculous mercy. He wore our rejection and identified with our exile and outsider status. All at once the cross speaks of love and forgiveness and invites us to come closer. "Father, forgive them, for they know not what they do!" (Luke 23:34) It is imperative that we the church see the world from the perspective of the cross, the same way that God sees the world. At its essence the cross is people oriented, and so must the church become.

There is no message that should be more compelling than the gospel and no haven from the storm more inviting than the church. It is more than a story; it is the ultimate story of God's passionate pursuit and reckless resolve to heal and restore everything that has been broken by sin. This is not just history; this is our story—each of us. For the church to be a light in the midst of this psuedo-connected society, we are going to have to turn our hearts and our attention to loving the way Jesus loves and making room for the orphan and the outsider. We are going to have to realize once and for all that our culture's greatest deficit is our greatest asset.

LADDER OF SUCCESS

Perhaps the greatest insight we have into God's intentions for the church is the story of Jacob. Born into the covenant and promises made to his grandfather Abraham, Jacob grew up in a home where he struggled with significance and identity. He was not the favorite son of his father, Isaac, and most of his life he lived in the shadow of his brother, Esau, just outside of his father's good graces. Isaac loved Esau more than he loved Jacob, and Jacob knew it. He turned to his mother for nurture, but there was a constant struggle taking place within him that dated all the way back to the womb where they competed for who would enter the world first. Jacob's name tells us everything we need know about him. It means "supplanter" and "deceiver." He desperately wanted to be loved and favored by his father, but it just didn't happen. He was the ultimate outsider and emotional exile.

Jacob lived most of his life in a state of frustration. The Bible describes him as a "quiet man, dwelling in tents" (Gen. 25:27). I think it's safe to say that Jacob spent a lot of time alone, thinking about his life and his future. He learned to manipulate in order to get what he wanted and what he believed had been kept from him. He tricked Esau into giving up his birthright, and he worked out a scheme with his mother to receive the blessing of the firstborn by taking advantage of his father's poor health and weakening vision. In the end he gained what he thought he wanted but at a high price.

He was forced to flee from his dysfunctional family and the anger of his brother, still broken on the inside without the ability to fix himself. It appeared that now he had lost everything in his pursuit to gain anything that would give him peace and sense of importance. Jacob is a perfect picture of many in this generation.

Carrying all of this deep internal turmoil, Jacob journeyed out into the world in pursuit of something that, to this point, he had not been able to find: meaning. Exhausted, he arrived in a desolate place and was forced to camp for the night. It was here in this lonely place, far from home and alone with his thoughts and baggage, that he received one of the greatest revelations ever recorded in the pages of Scripture.

As he slept, he dreamed of a stairway that reached from the earth up to heaven. And he saw the angels of God going up and down the stairway. At the top of the stairway stood the LORD, and he said, "I am the LORD, the God of your grandfather Abraham, and the God of your father, Isaac. The ground you are lying on belongs to you. I am giving it to you and your descendants.

Your descendants will be as numerous as the dust of the earth! They will spread out in all directions—to the west and the east, to the north and the south. And all the families of the earth will be blessed through you and your descendants. What's more, I am with you, and I will protect you wherever you go. One day I will bring you back to this land. I will not leave you until I have finished giving you everything I have promised you." Then Jacob awoke from his sleep and said, "Surely the LORD is in this place, and I wasn't even aware of it!" But he was also afraid and said, "What an awesome place this is! It is none other than the house of God, the very gateway to heaven!"

—GENESIS 28:12–17, NLT

Jacob's heart and imagination were supernaturally flooded with a vision and understanding of God's presence and good intentions for his life. For the first time his life made sense and God was "firsthand." The promises that God had made so long ago to his forefather were now his to own. They were no longer someone else's stories. They were his first by experience. God became a reality to Jacob, present even when He wasn't obvious.

This desolate place had previously been named Luz, but in that moment Jacob renamed it based on his life-changing encounter. Bethel, the house of God, now held a significant place in his journey to destiny. This X had now marked the spot where he had realized that the internal struggle and hunger that had driven him all of his life were not going to be met by external things or accomplishments. He no longer had to manipulate his way to greatness. That Bethel revelation had indelibly marked and defined his life and his future. Whether or not he was ever accepted back into his father's house or was received by his brother was no longer the barrier that kept him from belonging. He knew he was a part of God's household, and there was an open door to him and a stairway that gave him access to the giver of the promises.

I believe there are several facets of Jacob's dream that need to shape our vision of what the church, the house of God, must be to our Jacob-like generation—a generation that is equally dysfunctional and knows fatherlessness all too well, a generation that is fighting the same internal battle for significance and meaning, trying to find their place in the big picture, and a generation that has all the information it will ever need but is in desperate pursuit of a firsthand encounter with the living God that produces a three-dimensional faith.

> This is Jacob, the generation of those who seek Him, who seek Your face.
>
> —Psalm 24:6, NKJV

The Church as a Family

For the church to truly and effectively reflect the culture of heaven we must see ourselves as the family of God more than anything else. The unique revelation that Jacob received was centered around the presence of God as the "house" of God. For Jacob this was significant. He had never really felt "at home" in the tents of his father. Now while on a search for a home and a family of his own, God chose to reveal Himself in such a way that brought security, identity, and belonging to Jacob's soul. That is what a father does for a family, and it is what God does for us. He takes us, who are orphans, and adopts us and gives us the confidence that He is ever with us and available to us through the Holy Spirit within us.

For you did not receive the spirit of slavery to fall back
into fear, but you have received the Spirit of adoption
as sons, by whom we cry, "Abba, Father!" The Spirit
himself bears witness with our spirit that we are children of God.

—ROMANS 8:15–16

Acceptance, love, and a sense of being closely connected
to God and other people are basic human needs. God created us with these longings. Jacob's "homelessness" and
search for a father figure are something we all can relate
to. Some of us have witnessed firsthand how single-parent
homes and divorce devastate marriages and families. Many
people affected by these situations are forced to look beyond
bloodlines and last names to friends and coworkers as the
most significant people in their lives because of the incredible pain associated with their biological families.

One of the core needs for the twenty-first-century church
is to establish strong bonds of family and tribe. We can look
at the brokenness of the family structure within society and
decry it, or we can answer it by filling the void. There is not
another institution on the planet that is equally equipped
to offer a solution to this problem as much as the church
is. It has always been this way, but at times we have been
distracted from seeing what should be natural to us. As a
community that is built upon a passionate Father's love that
pulses for people, we should mirror this emotion by loving
people even when they least deserve it.

We need to be reminded that everyone is still "in process"
and relearn to have grace for one another, just as we desire.
Remember, no one is finished and no one is complete. No
family is perfect and no church will be either. What is most
important is not the perfection of the members but the perfection of God's process. I have told our staff over and over

again that if we ever get to the point where most of the people who attend our church are spiritually mature, then we are failing! That may seem odd, but the church, just like a family, must have parents and must also have children at different levels of development in order to be a healthy expression of fruitfulness. God is a loving Father who is developing and, at times, disciplining us all to bring us to a place of maturity. He is not an overbearing dictator with no patience for our process. He is the Lord of the process. A revelation of the love of God always orients us toward others. "We love because he first loved us" (1 John 4:19).

AN EXTRAORDINARY EXPERIENCE

Another aspect of being people oriented is creating an environment in which people from the outside are able to experience God's presence and reality in a new way. Jacob's response to the God-given dream was to say, "How awesome is this place!" This should be the goal of every church, for people to walk away from our church services, classes, outreaches, small groups, and chance encounters with members saying, "How awesome is this church!" I am not just talking about the external things that make a good performance or spectacular show, although we should do everything we do with a spirit of excellence. What I am referring to is the preparation of God's presence and our spirit of hospitality on display. The one thing that should mark the people of God as being different from any other people or place in this world is the manifest presence of God in our midst.

> "My presence will go with you, and I will give you rest." And he said to him, "If your presence will not go with me, do not bring us up from here. For how shall it be known that I have found favor in your sight, I and your people? Is it not in your going with

us, so that we are distinct, I and your people, from every other people on the face of the earth?"

—EXODUS 33:14–16

The presence of God is the only differentiator between communities and gatherings of earthly origin and the collective gathering of the church. That is the principle of the "gateway." The church is the access point to the realities of heaven here on earth.

Hollywood cannot imitate or compete with this supernatural environment with all of their best special effects and endless budgets. Wherever the manifest presence of the Lord is, the kingdom of God becomes accessible and the Holy Spirit is present to bring the kingdom agenda into a visible and experiential reality. Salvation, healing, conviction, boldness, faith, and restoration of everything and anything become an imminent possibility in this awesome place.

I fear that at times we have put too much confidence in our ability to manufacture environments that attract people with the mere tools of the marketplace and ignore our central mission as kings and priests to contend for the presence of God. I am not against the externals or aesthetics and the planning and programming that are necessary to be hospitable and even creative in our approach to doing church. But if we build great sets and structures but fail to remember the Lord's irreplaceable presence as the one thing that marks the church as *awesome*, we will relegate ourselves to irrelevance. The early church was marked by "awe and wonder" at the realization that God was in their midst. It became the rallying point that drew them together to study the Scriptures, pray and break bread, remembering what God was doing among them (Acts 2:42). It was what left those on the outside looking in, respectful and curious about this *new way*.

People are hungry for an encounter, an experience with the living God, especially this generation that is overloaded and overstimulated with information, entertainment, and the "bigger is better" phenomena. What they are starving for is community and a sense of the divine at work in their lives. The church must be the ladder that brings the reality of an awesome God to a world looking for a way to "taste and see" that the Lord is indeed "good." God has always had it in mind that even those who are outsiders and seekers would be drawn to His house. It's God's desire and should therefore be our design that there is a place in His house for them to encounter God in a way that brings joy and connection to their lives.

> Even them I will bring to My holy mountain, and make them joyful in My house of prayer. Their burnt offerings and their sacrifices will be accepted on my altar; for My house shall be called a house of prayer for all nations.
>
> —ISAIAH 56:7, NKJV

A PLACE IN THE STORY

Part of what it means for the church to be the *stairway* or *gateway* to heaven is to help people find the connection to the story of God. Jacob struggled to find his place in the covenant story that had defined his family all the way back to Abraham. All that God had revealed about Himself and all of the promises made to Abraham were generational, meaning they would be passed down to each of his descendants. Jacob's struggle from birth was centered in an attempt to find a way to inherit it these promises and heritage. From grabbling the heel of his twin, Esau, in the birth to the deception of his father to gain the blessing of the firstborn, Jacob was consumed with trying to find context for his life.

It was only in the place of Bethel, the house of God, that Jacob for the first time found his place in the story. It became his. God promised him in the same way that He had his grandfather Abraham that his descendants would be numerous and blessed. In essence God was telling Jacob, "You have a place and part in what I am doing in the earth. You belong!"

As the church we are guardians and tellers of the grandest of all stories. The gospel is not a new story but the continuation and the fulfillment of God's one and only story of redemption and rescue that began with Abraham and finds its completion in Jesus Christ. This story is not just the subject matter of our spiritual discussions on Sundays at church but also the central message of all history and destiny. It's bigger than anyone of us, but each of us must find our onramp into the story for it to come to life for us. The gospel becomes each of ours when we realize that this plan of God to rescue and redeem everything that had been lost included us. Our story intersects with God's salvation story, and by faith they become one.

As a pastor I have sat with countless people who can relate to this. They struggle to know what all of the stories and principles they read and hear from the Bible have to do with them. Many people are secretly bored or uninterested, biding time listening to sermons and singing songs in church. I believe that many times it is because we have not helped them see the bigger picture—that they are included in this massive story, that all of the people they read about are their relatives by faith and the promises remain for them as well.

One of the greatest moments as a pastor came for me last year when I was baptizing several new believers on a Sunday morning. Before we actually baptized them, we held a class and taught the history and the purpose of water baptism—of entering into the death, burial, and resurrection of Jesus. We taught them that they were joining into the body of Christ as millions of other believers on every continent and in every era of history have for two millennia. One particular young lady, a college student at our local university, had recently come to faith but was struggling with where she fit in and how she would live out this newfound faith.

After I had baptized her and the others and went back stage to pray with everyone, she approached me with wide eyes and said to me, "I get it now!" I asked her what she meant, and her answer brought tears to my eyes. She said, "When I went under the water I was immersed into the family of God. My disappointing past got overwhelmed by all of the huge victories of Jesus and the church before me. I'm not a loser anymore. I have a new name and a new story!" All I could say to her was, "Welcome to the family!"

Chapter 9

BE KINGDOM FOCUSED:
IN A SPIRITUALLY
BLINDED CULTURE

If we only had eyes to see and ears to hear and wits
to understand, we would know that the Kingdom of
God in the sense of holiness, goodness, beauty is as
close as breathing and is crying out to born both
within ourselves and within the world; we would
know that the Kingdom of God is what we all of
us hunger for above all other things even when we
don't know its name or realize that it's what we're
starving to death for.[1]

—FREDERICK BUECHNER

EVERAL YEARS AGO I found myself in a car accident
that didn't have to happen. I had left the church
office after a long day and had only one stop to make
before heading home. I was cruising down one of the main
roads in our town listening to a teaching tape (yes, I said
"tape") as I went along. I came to one of the busiest inter-
sections in our part of town and stopped at the red light
in the middle lane. While waiting for the light to turn, I
went to take out the current tape that had just finished and
replace it with the next in the teaching series. The cassette
fell from my hand into the floorboard of the passenger side
of the truck, just out of my reach. I leaned over carefully
with my foot firmly on the break pedal, trying to nudge the
cassette tape close enough to grab, all the while afraid I was
going to miss the light change.

At this point I must admit that I am somewhat of a nervous and aggressive driver. I don't like to be held up by slow drivers or drivers who don't understand the purpose of a passing lane. I especially hate it when people don't pay attention to the light changing and stay put as if it is still red. In this moment I was getting more nervous because I absolutely knew that the light was about to immediately turn green. I could barely see what was taking place in my peripheral vision, but I caught a glimpse of cars moving just outside the passenger side window. Just about that time I heard a car honk behind me, and I just knew I was holding up traffic. I reacted.

Instinctively I came up from my slouched position and gunned the gas of my Dodge Durango to get out of everybody's way. Boom! Before I could stop, before I even took a look at what was in front of me, I crashed into the car in front of me that had not moved (that is until I helped it move) and was still waiting for the light to change.

I had hit this car with such impact that the battery from under my hood was propelled through the air and onto the road. The rear of this vehicle was smashed beyond recognition, and radiator fluid was spraying everywhere. I could not believe I had made such an error in judgment. It was one of those moments when you wish you could turn back the clock. Little did I know that the situation was about to get just a little bit worse and a lot more interesting.

The passengers in the vehicle I had just mangled emerged from their car. Two huge men came walking back toward me swearing and lighting me up verbally in a manner to which I am unaccustomed. Both of them were wearing the identical black T-shirts with huge, white block letters stretched across their chest: P-O-L-I-C-E.

I had just smashed into an undercover, unmarked police car with two officers who were just pulling out of a fast-food restaurant on their way to a drug bust that they had been working on for over a year. Both of them were now wearing their lunch and less than happy with me. Their attitude lightened up a bit when they found out that I was a minister (one of them called me "Father," which I allowed at this point). I was eventually given a ticket for reckless driving and endured the embarrassment of standing there while onlookers pointed and laughed at me for over an hour. Finally I watched as my truck was towed away, and I waited for a ride from a friend.

The moral to this story? Losing your focus can be a very dangerous and costly thing to do, and what we think is true is not always so.

Staying Inside the Yellow Lines

The church, made up of living members, is the only expression of the kingdom of God that the world is able to see. They see the nature of God, experience the love of God, and draw their impressions of how God is from what they see in you and me. Because this is true, we must be diligent and intentional in keeping our focus sharp and confirming that the picture we are presenting to the world is an accurate one. Jesus succinctly described the religious leaders of His day as the blind leading the blind who lead themselves and their followers into a ditch (Matt. 15:14). We have to make sure that we are not shipwrecking ourselves and others by becoming distracted from the central focal point Jesus has called us to, the kingdom of God, and this call requires a continual realignment of our priorities and perspectives.

Staying with the vehicle/travel theme, imagine the church on a long journey. We have punched the address of our desired destination into the GPS system, and it is directing our movements and letting us know when to turn next. As we travel down the expressway toward our destination, even though we know the general direction and timing of our journey, we must still keep our vehicle between the yellow lines and out of the ditches to the right or the medium to the left. Maintaining proper alignment, which will get us to our destination, requires focus, perception, and thousands of constant, minor adjustments to keep us on the straight and narrow. If we focus too much upon the future or stare too long in the rear view mirror of the past, we will end up in the ditch of error or lose our focus completely. This idea of "alignment" is an appropriate picture of the work we must do to keep ourselves focused as children of the light in the midst of a world gone dark.

> Therefore do not be anxious, saying, "What shall we eat?" or "What shall we drink?" or "What shall we wear?" For the Gentiles seek after all these things, and your heavenly Father knows that you need them all. *But seek first the kingdom of God and his righteousness*, and all these things will be added to you.
> —MATTHEW 6:31–34, EMPHASIS ADDED

Jesus was crystal clear in giving to us the true north to align our every movement: the kingdom of God. He called us to move our eyes off of needs, wants, and the immediacy of crisis that is a constant in our daily experience and zoom our attention upon the reign and the rule of God. This is a more difficult task than it may sound, because the kingdom of God isn't visible to the naked eye, as some road sign or landmark off in the distant that we can easily see and orient ourselves by. In fact, the only ones who have the ability to even see or perceive this kingdom are those who have been born again by the Spirit of God and given new eyes to see.

Keeping our focus requires us knowing clearly what is and isn't true about the kingdom of God so that we will not easily become distracted by the shifting mirages that play tricks on our eyes, shifting images in our blind spots, calling for our attention off the road in front of us. Historically when the church has become lazy in keeping our focus, we fall prey to sly deceptions about what the kingdom of God is and isn't. This double vision has brought disaster upon the heart and effectiveness of the church in its mission to be the light of the world. During some of the darkest periods of history for the church we built hierarchal systems that bring people into bondage instead of freedom, declared war upon people of other religions over turf and territory, and falsely identified political party platforms as the means to transform culture instead of the salt and light of the gospel. We have turned inward our focus and battled to the death with one another over minor theological differences and divided ourselves with denominational labels instead of doing and being agents of the kingdom, united together in Christ. (By the way, the word *denomination* is defined as "to divide, to denominate.") We have at times become corrupted by all of the things Jesus warned us not to become "concerned" about and, in the process, lost sight of what the kingdom is really all about.

And the results speak for themselves. Fewer and fewer unchurched people express confidence in the church's integrity, attendance is decreasing year after year, and our cities continue to be taken over by crime, injustice, and immorality. Young people are being converted by the evangelists of Hollywood to a secular worldview, and all too often the church explains its ineffectiveness away as the result of the end times, eschatological apostasy, or people's hardness of heart toward Jesus.

I believe the church's best days are still ahead. I am not

a hater of the church; I am a fan. I have invested my life and everything I have into the life and mission of the local church because I am convinced that the plan and purpose of God for this world, in this generation, is going to be accomplished through a "radiant church, without stain or wrinkle" (Eph. 5:27, NIV). But for the church to move beyond our current state of passivity and toward our destiny of shining forth the light so brightly that it cannot be ignored, we are going to have to refocus our eyes upon the kingdom, what it is and what it isn't. Because, as I said earlier, becoming distracted is a very costly and dangerous thing to do. Just like a driver who finds himself in unfamiliar territory, sometimes we need to break out the maps and pull off the side of the road momentarily in order to regain our bearings and reorient ourselves toward our destination.

THE KINGDOM MISUNDERSTOOD

A big part of the problem is that there are so many various understandings of what the kingdom of God is and isn't. Because the concept of the kingdom is spiritually perceived and "not of this world" (speaking of origin, not location), it can also become the breeding ground for deception and misunderstanding that leads to confusion and frustration. Just as darkness grows in the absence of light, deception, as spiritual bacteria, expands and infects the church's mindset of the kingdom of God, producing all kinds of diseases in the body. The Bible is clear that what we don't know can and does hurt us: "My people are destroyed for lack of knowledge" (Hosea 4:6). Ignorance is the companion of deception.

Some assume that the kingdom of God is just referring to heaven or, more specifically, the afterlife. They believe that God only reigns in heaven, since that's where His throne is.

They don't have any application for how God could possibly rule in the here and now of earth. If this is our paradigm, we interpret Jesus's words to "seek first the kingdom" as an admonition to make sure we are "saved" so that when we die, we go to heaven (fire insurance), or to merely think about life from the perspective of a future heaven or hell. With a blurry perspective of the kingdom we reduce the gospel to the invisible reality separated from this physical reality. While both of these outcomes are positive and should be something that each believer should do, it is incomplete at best. It has no direct impact upon how we view our lives here and now or the things that we do with our lives.

To see the kingdom of God as only being futuristic causes the church to surrender our place of influence with our culture.

Some see the kingdom as limited to an earthly reign of Jesus as Israel's Messiah, taking place during the millennial reign from Jerusalem at the end of the world. Until then the world is under the government of the Satan, and the church is holding on and hiding out. They read the Book of Revelation only as futuristic and see this present world as something to endure until the future kingdom arrives. To speak of the kingdom as being present already is confusing to them, because if the kingdom was truly here now, wouldn't things be different? Wouldn't there be an end to sickness and disease? Wouldn't the devil be banished and wars come to an end?

This system of belief fails to see the tension between the kingdom as now and not yet. While it is true that Jesus will bring with Him the finality of the kingdom, the church is already aware of and experiencing the fullness of the kingdom now.

> For the kingdom of God is not a matter of eating and drinking but of righteousness and peace and joy in the Holy Spirit.
>
> —ROMANS 14:17

This view is formed typically around a dispensational understanding of the Scriptures. It has the potential of stealing the power and the motivation from the church to be salt and light engaging the principalities and powers hiding in darkness now in anticipation of Jesus's return. There is a yet another perspective of the kingdom that has emerged in the church recently. It is not necessarily a new slant as much as a recycled, hipper version of an old distortion. A variety of voices have emerged in the church that have become disgruntled with the old guard of leadership that has failed to address injustices connected to social issues such as poverty, climate change, and third world crisis. Many of them have also become leery of what they have seen done in the name of Christian media and some of the excesses connected with it. In response to what they view as an unacceptable portrayal of the kingdom of God by the church of the previous generation, they have shifted further left and defined kingdom work as only about social justice. While there is much virtue in addressing the needs of the poor, becoming better stewards of the planet, and being involved in political activism, we must be careful not to throw the baby out with the bathwater. This is only one facet of the kingdom of God and not the total picture.

We must enter into the fray on these issues if we are going to truly *be radiant,* but we have to view them from the vantage point of the larger kingdom and not forget the overall reality of the kingdom of God that transcends just addressing these issues as any other nonprofit would. We represent Jesus to the world, and we bring the power of the kingdom to bear upon the present before our King actually appears. We are the announcement of His reign, and we call everyone to bow the knee to Jesus as we demonstrate His grace and goodness. But make no mistake about it, Jesus will not be satisfied being one voice among many who are part of the global community addressing issues in a bland, nondescript, unoffending manner. The statues of Dagon will fall on their faces and be ground to dust at the name of Jesus.[2]

In order to keep kingdom focused as we journey toward our destiny to be salt and light, we must have a clear understanding of what the kingdom really is.

A MESSAGE TO BE ANNOUNCED

This is the message that Jesus began His ministry announcing. The good news that Jesus brought was that there is a regime change taking place. In the gospel Jesus preached, the old ruler, the devil, is put on notice and Jesus declares Himself the representative, the rightful King, superior in power who has invaded the territory of darkness and oppression to right every wrong.

> But if it is by the finger of God that I cast out demons, then the kingdom of God has come upon you. When a strong man, fully armed, guards his own palace, his goods are safe; but when one stronger than he attacks him and overcomes him, he takes away his armor in which he trusts and divides his spoil.
>
> —LUKE 11:20–22

Everything that Jesus did in healing the sick, casting out devils, confronting the establishment, and feeding the hungry was a sign to verify that His kingdom was more powerful and taking over. This announcement of the kingdom of

God was also a call to repent, or change the way of thinking, as a result of this announcement. Things were going to be different now that God's government had broken through the darkness of human history. The light was shining and a new creation was underway. The occupying enemies would ultimately lose power through the sacrificial and substitutionary death of the King Himself. He would prove His supremacy over all the forces of this malevolent dictator by defeating his ultimate tool of control—death itself. The Resurrection was both the deposing of the tyrant kingdom of darkness and the coronation of the King of all kings. This is the gospel of the kingdom, and it is the message that the church is commissioned to proclaim.

It's important that we understand that the connection between the kingdom of God and the gospel is inseparable. In much of the Western church the gospel has been reduced down to a therapeutic method to remove guilt for our sins and secure salvation in the afterlife. It has been stripped of its subversive implications. If God is not King "now," He has no power or authority to deliver from the power or authority of darkness. Historically the word *gospel* was connected with a herald carrying the vital message of a new Caesar/king coming to power throughout the streets of the empire.[3] The church needs to regain a perspective of Jesus as more than just the One who saved us from our sins but as King of the world with all authority in heaven and earth.

> All authority in heaven and earth has been given to me. Go therefore and make disciples of all nations, baptizing them in the name of the Father and of the Son and of the Holy Spirit.
>
> —MATTHEW 28:18–19

A DIMENSION TO BE ENTERED

The kingdom of God is essentially spiritual in nature because God is spirit. That does not mean that it is removed from the physical realm. To the contrary, everything that exists in the natural realm was created out of and is sustained by the eternal dimension, which is spiritual. (See Hebrews 11:6; Colossians 1:16–17.) Jesus said that His kingdom was not originated from the world and that it was not necessarily observable geographically, but it was from another world or realm.

> My kingdom is not of this world, If my kingdom were of this world, my servants would have been fighting, that I might not be delivered over to the Jews. But my kingdom is not from this world.
>
> —JOHN 18:36

> Nor will they say, "Look, here it is!" or "There!" for behold, the kingdom of God is in the midst of you.
>
> —LUKE 18:21

Jesus said that the kingdom was all around us, imminent and invisible to the naked eye. It cannot be entered or grasped with natural senses or means. The kingdom of God is not so much an issue of geography or methodology as much as it is about cardiology. It must be entered by faith since "faith is the substance of things hoped for, the evidence of things not seen" (Heb. 11:1, NKJV). Jesus was clear that the only way for us to ever "see" or understand God's kingdom was to be born again by the Spirit of God.

> "Truly, truly, I say to you, unless one is born again he cannot see the kingdom of God." Nicodemus said to him, "How can a man be born when he is old? Can

he enter a second time into his mother's womb and be born?" Jesus answered, "Truly, truly, I say to you, unless one is born of water and Spirit, he cannot enter the kingdom of God."

—John 3:3–5

The kingdom of God is available and constantly overlapping our present reality and experience. It is a tangible environment that is not obvious to those who aren't aware of it or looking for it, but it is capable of altering anything and everything in this present realm that is contrary to the will of God. My good friend Bob Hamp has written an incredible book, *Think Differently, Live Differently*. In this book he describes the environmental aspect of the kingdom in this way:

> The kingdom of God is a spiritual Kingdom and therefore invisible to the human eye. It is a Kingdom whose atmosphere is love because Pure Love rules, not just an attitude but as a conquering force. The atmosphere is righteousness, not because a rigid set of doctrines are adhered to by the force of will but because righteousness flows out of accurate perceptions. The atmosphere is life, not just as the opposite of death but as the force of aliveness that conquers not only death, but sickness, depression and every other thing that would try to drain the life from God's sons and daughters.[4]

Faith comes when the Word, or the message of the kingdom, comes and opens our heart to the present reality of God's rightful rule and gives us the ability to experience a resurrection of our souls unto eternal life. That's why to some the Bible and Christianity just don't seem to make any sense to them. They are trying to figure God out with their natural minds and logic to the point where it becomes too painful, too unrealistic, or too offensive for them to believe that all of this time "the world...has been pulled over their eyes to blind [them] from the truth."[5]

> In their case the god of this world has blinded the minds of the unbelievers, to keep them from seeing the light of the gospel of the glory of Christ, who is the image of God.
>
> —2 CORINTHIANS 4:4

AN INHERITANCE TO BE RECEIVED

It is the Holy Spirit who gives us insight to understand and become familiar as new citizens of this kingdom reality. He illuminates our hearts to see the truth about God, the world, and our identity. It teaches us the way things really work. It is by revelation that we become convinced and able to enter and possess the kingdom of God as our inheritance (Eph. 1:18–19).

In order for us to stay focused in our pursuit of God's kingdom to come and His will to be done as Jesus taught us to pray (Matt. 6:10), we must keep in mind that all of the things that seem so valuable in this world are fading away and rubbish compared to the riches of the kingdom.

The greatest tool that the enemy possesses to get our eyes off of the treasure that we are receiving in the kingdom is to offer a more immediate alternative of worldly origin. Jesus described these distracting sirens as "thorns" that choke out the good news of the kingdom and keep us from being fruitful (Luke 8:14). Position and power, things that riches can buy and carnal pleasures offer immediate gratification and a false sense of belonging and security (1 John 2:15–17).

The Bible calls us to be thankful that in the midst of this world that is falling apart and constantly shifting in instability, we are receiving a kingdom that is secure, solid, and holds the promise of reward both now and in the future age to come.

> Therefore let us be grateful for receiving a kingdom that cannot be shaken, and thus let us offer to God acceptable worship, with reverence and awe, for our God is a consuming fire.
> —Hebrews 12:28–29

Worship and faithful prayer are the currency of the kingdom. We don't have to wait for the Second Coming before we pray as if we were already reigning with Him, because we are. We don't have to wait for heaven until we worship as if there are a myriad of angels and the elect already enamored by His glory, because they are. We don't have to tolerate the onslaught of the enemy's accusations because we are already redeemed and cleanse and adopted into the royal family of God.

Compromise is always a temptation the devil uses against God's children to keep them from receiving the totality of their inheritance. He offered the shortcut to Jesus, and he will to you as well. Too many Christians settle for the immediate and the temporal joy that comes from living lukewarm because they have failed to realize that the reward of the kingdom is available for them to inherit today. The kingdom of God is at hand!

POWER TO BE DEMONSTRATED

The kingdom is more than just a message or a new way to look at things through the lens of religion. It is God's rule and reality inaugurated by Jesus and now expanding in this present world. It is not a secret to be kept but "good news" that comes with certain indicators and signs of its presence already at work.

Paul said that when he came to Corinth, he didn't just come preaching these principles, but he also came with a demonstration of power to verify the authenticity of this message (1 Cor. 2:4–5). This is one of the distinctives of the gospel over other messages. Since the gospel of Jesus's kingdom declares that things as they have been (broken by sin and hijacked by the devil) are not the way God intended them to be and will not be tolerated any longer, demonstration is one of the ways God displays His greater power and authority.

The church needs a new demonstration of the Spirit that announces the presence of the kingdom in our midst to the world. Jesus said that the anointing that was upon Him was to preach good news *and* bring liberty to captives, open blind eyes, and deliver the oppressed (Luke 4:18–19). It was both.

We do not live in an era in which people are free from all bondage and oppression. We still see sickness and disease wreaking havoc on people the world over. There is as much or more demonization taking place as there ever has been. Mental illness and depression are at epidemic proportions, and the medical field is running out of answers. It is not as though this world no longer needs a demonstration of the power of God. It needs it perhaps now more than ever. Every time we see the miraculous breaking into this present age, it is like a welcome road sign along the highway that reminds us that we are moving in the right direction and our destination is growing ever closer.

If we become too sophisticated and intellectual in our approach to the gospel and the kingdom of God, we may fall prey to the temptation to relegate the supernatural to another time. Many have tried to explain anything supernatural in the Bible as either myth or a pre-enlightenment attempt at explaining complex mental and emotional phenomena. There is no devil. Healing is all based upon the power of suggestion, and there are no angels or miracles, only science and doctrine.

I believe if we are to engage our culture with an authentic presentation of Jesus as King, then we will need an equally authentic demonstration of power that defeats darkness and brings answers and freedom in places that the wisdom of men has failed to succeed.

A LIFESTYLE TO BE IMITATED

Finally, the kingdom is chiefly expressed through the citizens of the kingdom demonstrating the new ethic of "Thy kingdom come." What does it mean to be a Christian? That is a question that is answered so many different ways today. Some would define it by a prayer that is prayed or a building that is attended. Some would describe it in terms of sacraments observed or intellectual principles subscribed to. While all of these are great *descriptions of* a Christian, they are poor *definitions*. This is the essence of what a Christian is: a follower of Jesus Christ in the Jesus way.

After all, isn't this what Jesus invited each of His original disciples to do—"Follow Me"? It was a call to leave an old life behind and to learn a new way, the way of the Cross and Resurrection.

> To follow Jesus implies that we enter into a way of life that is given character and shape and direction by the one who calls us. To follow Jesus means picking up rhythms and ways of doing things that are often unsaid but always derivative from Jesus, formed by the influence of Jesus. To follow Jesus means that we can't separate what Jesus is saying from what Jesus is doing and the way he is doing it. To follow Jesus is as much, or maybe even more about feet as it is about ears and eyes.[6]

As people of dual citizenship (kingdom of God and this world) we are called to willfully imitate the lifestyle of the kingdom that we find in following Jesus. Following requires close observation, study, and thoughtful paying attention that leads us to imitation. That's how we learn; we watch others and imitate what we see, as frustrating as it is to learn a "new way," until we develop muscle memory and it becomes second nature (or primary nature).

It's much like learning a new language. Even though I took Spanish and Latin in high school for four years, I cannot speak either well. I can pick up a word here or there and some things sound familiar to me, but it is painfully slow and sporadic. English is the language I think in and communicate with.

My good friend John Vereecken is a missionary in Latin America. He and his wife have been in Mexico for more than twenty-five years and now are used to influence churches and leaders across all of Spanish-speaking Latin America. When he moved to Mexico, he could not speak Spanish, but he immediately immersed himself in the language and the culture until he became fluent. Over the course of twenty-plus years Spanish has become his primary language because he has immersed himself. He studied others and followed their example. Now he thinks in Spanish and has to translate back into English even though for the first half of his life English was his main language. Now it is more difficult for him to speak it than it is for him to communicate and think in Spanish and the Latin culture.

What's the difference between John and me? We both took Spanish classes and both practiced, but John immersed himself into the language and culture as a student and follower. I observed and gave it minimal attention but clung to my English and even tried to learn Spanish through my English-speaking American filter.

This is a perfect picture of the way we are called to imitate and demonstrate the lifestyle and culture of the kingdom of God in the midst of this broken and blinded world. Following Jesus is a call to abandon the life (in the land of death) and embrace a new way, a new language, and a new culture. How do we do this when we have never been to this new country? We follow and imitate the way of the One who personifies the kingdom of heaven and brought it to us here on earth.

Jesus taught us about the culture of the kingdom in what has become known as the Sermon on the Mount. This teaching wasn't just to teach an ideal that could never be met or a philosophy that we were unable to live out. It was the ethic of heaven. Jesus lived this perfectly in front of all of us, even to the point of dying in His innocence by the hands of the guilty. He ultimately defeated the power of sin and death at the cross and inaugurated the new creation plan of the Father at the Resurrection.

The nine Beatitudes and the rest of the instruction that Jesus taught us in the sermon describe the intention of God for the new humanity, not just a prescripted list of dos and don'ts or a perfect ethic that somehow man is capable of attaining with the right level of discipline. The broken world needs rescue, and our broken souls are the starting point but not the finish line of salvation. How we treat others, resolve conflict, and respond to mistreatment are all triggers that continue to set off the destructive course of violence, retribution, and sinful devastation regardless of time or place. Issues of the heart and soul require a turnover of regime and a commitment to receive and learn a new language and culture. That is the meaning of repentance: to change our thinking in such a way that we live differently. Our destination is the kingdom, and it can only be "seen" and "entered" with the aid of the Holy Spirit.

Jesus gave us both His life and teaching as an illustrated model of how the kingdom looks on the earth through the lives of willing citizens, filled with the power and perspective of heaven. He showed us how this kingdom culture could be expressed through the lives of men and women who are more saturated and immersed in the kingdom of God than the ways and means of this current world system that is dominated and dictated by the devil and demonic powers. We must become apprentices who study and follow, imitate and become skilled by grace at living the kingdom way in the here and now. N. T. Wright states it this way:

> Those who follow Jesus can begin to practice, in the present, the habits and life which correspond to the way things are in God's kingdom—the way they will be eventually, yes, but also the way they *already* are because Jesus is here.[7]

Of course this isn't something we do in our own strength. It begins when the Holy Spirit, the earnest and guarantee of our future completed redemption, brings the life of God within us, empowering us to live this new way. He comes to lead us into all truth and teach us how to walk as Jesus did. This is what Jesus meant when He said He would not leave us as orphans. We read the Scriptures, study Jesus, and allow the Holy Spirit to mentor us as we learn to follow Jesus and speak the language of the kingdom.

As He Is

We are called to be the light of this world; just as Jesus was in His humanity, now He is shining through His followers. The lights go on for a world that has been shrouded in the darkness of selfishness and self-seeking when our lives look different to them. When kindness, compassion, and goodness are our pattern of living, it contrasts against the grain and testifies to the reality that something is different and something has changed. A major paradigm adjustment is needed for the church to cease seeing salvation through our own lens and realize that there are others watching. We receive the life and nature of God inwardly at salvation, but we must give the life and love of God outward from our salvation.

God came "to us" to be "God with us" and then "God in us" so that ultimately He could express "God through us." Please don't hear me saying that somehow we have the potential to somehow metamorphasize into gods in some erroneous way. There is only one God. But God has taken up His abode within the temple of His church and dwells behind the veil of our hearts and lives. We must see ourselves as carriers of the same kingdom chromosome we see in the life of Jesus. The apostle John wrote to us:

…because as he is *so also are we* in this world.

—1 JOHN 4:17, EMPHASIS ADDED

Our ability to demonstrate the light of God's goodness and nature to a world that is spiritually blind and groping in darkness will be found in our consistent commitment to being "followers of the Jesus way." They have seen our advertisements, heard our sermons, followed our bumper stickers, and visited our churches. They want to see God the way He is and know that He is present today. The more we follow Jesus, the more we think in "kingdom." The more we think and imitate what we see in Jesus and read in Scripture, the more it will be expressed through our lives. With every brush stroke of words, prayers, and actions that demonstrates the kingdom of God already here in us, the clearer the picture becomes and the brighter the light shines, filling the world with the light of hope.

Chapter 10

BE MISSION MOTIVATED:
IN A CLIMATE OF APATHY

I have but one candle of life to burn, and I would
rather burn it out in a land filled with darkness than
in a land flooded with light.[1]
　　—JOHN KEITH FALCONER, SCOTTISH MISSIONARY

The mission of the church is missions.[2]
　　　　　　　—OSWALD J. SMITH

AS THE EIGHTEENTH century was breaking across
the European continent, a young man of noble
heritage was entering onto history's scene. Niko-
laus von Zinzendorf came into the world at a time when the
once hot fires of the Protestant Reformation that had reig-
nited a passion for the cause of Christ throughout most of
Europe had now dwindled to mere embers. The church had
once again forgotten its first love and was quickly fossil-
izing into a hardened monument to the days gone by. It had
become institutionalized, ceasing to be a movement aflame
to fulfill its mission, even to the point of persecuting those
who would dare contend for a biblical emphasis upon world
evangelism, biblical unity, and unfettered personal devotion
to Jesus.

In his youth it was obvious that Zinzendorf was more
drawn to theology and the pursuit of a deeper knowledge of
God than to the subjects that might be expected of someone
whose family were wealthy aristocrats and land barons.[3] As
a nobleman it was expected that he, like his father, would

make politics his career and take his place among those of equal standing. But after just a short period of time of serving in the government, he was completely dissatisfied and dreamed of using his influence and wealth to further the cause of Christ. He seized what he viewed as a "God opportunity" to purchase an estate, Berthelsdorf, [4] from his aged grandmother with the intent that he would live there and build a community of refuge for persecuted believers. Within a short time of making this property available, refugees from the Moravian movement desperate for relief from the heat of persecution arrived at the count's doorstep having heard of his generous offer and passion for Christ. Very quickly a community grew, and Zinzendorf began his holy experiment.

The Moravians established their colony on the Zinzendorf's estate and renamed it Herrnhut, or the "Lord's Watch." Soon the population of Herrnhut began to swell, and community life was developing around the studying of Scripture and a lifestyle of constant prayer. Almost six hundred Moravians had joined Herrnhut at its height, and Count Zinzendorf's kindness and obvious passion and charisma elevated him to a place of leadership among their ranks.

One thing that bothered Zinzendorf and gripped his heart throughout his years growing up within the traditional Lutheran church was the general apathy of Christians toward prayer and missions. He knew of the opulent wealth of those who sat week in and week out in the services and yet did next to nothing to advance the cause of Christ beyond the stained-glass windows of their church buildings. He felt that the messages were stale and lifeless and accounted for much of this malaise to a growing apathy that had somehow infected the established church from the clergy on down the ranks. He was confounded at how the church that had begun with the Ninety-Five Theses of

Luther's protest against corruption and callousness could itself now become contaminated with the same sickness. Most of those who had joined him at Herrnhut had themselves experienced intense persecution due mostly to their pursuit of a religion of the heart over their intellect. Pietism was the official target of the institutional church's angst, and all who would dare speak of God in personal terms or suggest that the church was failing in its mission were subject to severe punishment.

The piety and the passion of the Moravians began to convict and shape Zinzendorf more than he had planned, and for the first time in his life he felt that he was in the company of true followers of Jesus. He felt a sense of hope and optimism that they may be able to restoke the coals of passion for Christ and His cause that had waned throughout Europe and bring about a new reformation from their small nucleus.

In August of 1727, after a season of working through some issues that were causing disunity to emerge, Zinzendorf led a prayer meeting and Communion service in which a spirit of repentance and conviction fell upon those who were gathered. Their hearts were knit together in unity, and the presence of God was so tangible that they refused to end the prayer meeting that would be labeled as the "Moravian Pentecost."[5] Instead they decided to keep it going around the clock, taking turns ministering to the Lord in a relay of prayer. By the count's later admission, signs, wonders, and miracles from heaven occurred in the midst of their prayer gatherings, and they were all plastered to this holy altar of prayer. The greatest miracle that took place was the gift of holy hunger and a renewed passion for world evangelism. They had stumbled upon this divine encounter and were committed that they were not going to allow the "fire to go out" upon the altar of the Lord. This prayer meeting endured 24/7 for over one hundred years and is looked upon as a catalyst for one of the greatest missionary movements the world has ever seen!

Eventually many of this community of Herrnhut would go to the farthest corners of the world as missionaries, never to return to their homelands. Some even went to the extent of selling themselves as slaves in order to bring the gospel to the slaves of the West Indies. There was no other alternative except to become *incarnational* in their approach and identify with those in chains in order to bring light to the darkest places on earth.

It is reported that as the first few men, who had forsaken comfort and family and intentionally indentured themselves, were about to set sail into the unknown, they spoke these last words from the deck of their ship to their friends and families: "May the Lamb that was slain receive the rewards of His suffering!"[6] This became the cry of the Moravians and many radicals after them.

WHAT HAPPENS TO US?

Why is it that the central mission of the church to "go" seemingly loses steam in each successive generation? It seems that this should be simple for the church to grasp. We read the words in red, seek the face of God, and unite together to win for the Lamb the rewards of His suffering. After all, isn't this what Jesus died for—to save the world? Isn't this why Jesus has empowered us with the Holy Spirit—to win the world and demonstrate the superiority of His kingdom? Then what is the root cause of our passivity?

This isn't always true. It seems that God raises up new voices and a fresh prophetic call for the church to join with God in His mission to rescue and to save. Then the momentum that the prophetic voice helps to create begins to slow down again until it comes to a stall. It's as if the wineskin of the church that is meant to carry the wine and the oil of the gospel has a leak in it that takes a generation to discover. As the legendary missionary David Livingston once said, "This generation can only reach this generation."[7]

If there has ever been a generation that has had the great task and opportunity that this one has, I am unaware of it. There are more people alive on the planet today than there has ever been. In fact, if you were to add up all the people who have ever lived, it still would not equal the number of people alive today. There are more believers alive today. We have a rich heritage from those who have gone before us and their testimonies and sacrifice to set the stage. We have more money, more information, and greater learning than ever before. We live in a generation that has the ability to travel, communicate, and reach more people than ever before in history. Literally the greatest harvest that the world has ever witnessed can take place in a single generation if only the church will give it our complete focus and resources. We could also neglect this moment in history and miss our day of visitation. What a tragedy that would be. I do not believe God will allow this to happen, and even now He is stirring and fanning the flames in the hearts of His people. This is a divine setup and ambush of grace for each of us.

We lose our oil of passion ever so slowly, and before we know it, we have become indifferent and apathetic toward what God's heart burns for. It's like a boiling kettle upon the stove. As long as the flame is kept constant and burning, the water continues to boil and the whistle blows. Turn the heat down or extinguish the flame, and the call ceases and the water cools.

There is a constant correlation between the church's passion for missions and our ceaseless pursuit of the God in intercessory prayer. You can find this pattern in every generation and every revival throughout church history. When we seek the heart of the Lamb, we become burning flames ablaze for what is aflame within the heart of the Lamb. When we become complacent in our prayers toward heaven, we will see this reflected in our apathy for the nations of the world. Make no mistake about it; the chief reason you and I exist is to partner together as the people of God, empowered by His Spirit, to fulfill the Jesus mission until He comes. Everything else is peripheral. Everything else is a limb branching off from the trunk of the Great Commission. The church, made up of each of us as unique members, is here in our generation to bring the light of God to people and places that are still hidden under spiritual darkness and ignorance, telling and demonstrating that Jesus is Lord!

In order for the church of the twenty-first century to be radiant, we must fight against the apathy of this age and contend for the core simplicity of the gospel.

> Besides this you know the time, that the hour has come for you to awake from sleep. For salvation is nearer to us now than when we first believed. The night is far gone; the day is at hand. So then let us cast off the works of darkness and put on the armor of light.
>
> —ROMANS 13:11–12

We must be cautious never to allow the gospel, once and for all delivered to the saints, to become watered down, redefined, shelved for others, or allowed to become something outdated. If the fact that so many billions of people on this planet still have never heard and so many within our own American culture have heard an erroneous gospel does not shake us to the core and drive us to pray, I fear we only have ashes to look forward to.

I believe that the Holy Spirit is blowing upon the coals of this generation and awakening a passionate breed of Jesus followers who will become radical in their willingness to do whatever it takes to win the nations of this world. The trappings of this world that are designed to lull us to sleep will have no allure because our lamps have become filled to overflowing with a passion for our Jesus, our Lamb, and His cause. This can be a generation of extravagant worship, ceaseless prayer, and reckless abandonment to "go" in the marketplace, the media, and all the other mountains of influence but with a single devotion to the kingdom of God. What will that look like? Let's consider what must change in our paradigms in order to become a mission-motivated, prayer-fueled, radiant church ready to seize the opportunity to reach our generation.

MISSION-MOTIVATED PEOPLE

The first mind-set that must change is our viewpoint of "who" is called. Most Christians, consciously or unconsciously, believe that only a very few are called to be missionaries. I believe this is why some Christians struggle with boredom in their walk. They don't understand that they were created on purpose for a mission. Being an imitator of Christ is the whole idea of what a Christian is. This is why Jesus's followers were eventually called Christians—they were imitating what Jesus had done and were called "little Christs."

Jesus Christ was the first missionary. He was sent from heaven, became one of us in order to identify with us, and eventually gave His life for us. He was God made "visible," and He came looking for us to save us. Earth was His mission field, and He was motivated only to serve the mission of His father (John 5:30).

If Jesus is our model to imitate, then we by definition are all missionaries, called and sent to become the Word, or message, made human for all to see. We each have a mission field, or a lamp stand, where God has uniquely designed us to be placed. We have been placed there to shine and give light to who God is and what He is like. Every one of us is a missionary. This is what it means to be a follower of Jesus, our Lamb. Wherever He is going, we are following, and Jesus is still going to the dark places—the voids, the destitute, the broken, the untold, the hurting, and those who have not had an opportunity to bow their knee to His lordship. If we are going in any other direction than where Jesus is going, we are failing to follow and are walking away from where His heart is compelled to go. Since God is a mission-motivated God and Jesus is a mission-motivated Savior, His followers must be mission-motivated people.

Every believer must have a renewed understanding that we are all kings and priests, given the vocation to be the light of the world. We are tentmakers—working jobs, raising families, and living lives that are all part of the platform that God has created for us. When we begin to see ourselves and everything in our lives as a tool to win the lost, it changes our perspective. We are no longer just fulfilling an obligation; we are now living our lives with the purpose of bringing light to a dark world becoming our grand obsession, privilege, and calling.

Every time we give our tithes and offerings or support missions projects, plant churches, or bring relief to the poor in Jesus's name, we are becoming the Word made flesh. Say it with me, "I am a missionary, sent by God to my generation, to win for the Lamb the rewards of His suffering!" The great revivalist and missionary John Wesley stated what should be our attitude toward money in this life, "Not, how much of my money will I give God, but how much of God's money will I keep for myself!"[8]

WHAT IS A MISSION FIELD?

Traditionally the American church has viewed missions as something that is done by a select group of radicals who move to remote places on the globe that we call "the field." The problem with that perspective in today's culture is that many of those nations, where missionaries were needed in the past, actually have more Christians and a more vibrant expression of the faith than we do now here in North America. Not in any way am I saying that the job is done and that there are no longer any unreached people groups or areas on the globe left to hear the gospel—to the contrary. But if we were to simply evaluate the size of the mission need by simple population of the untold, the unchurched, and non-Christians, North America would be in the top-five largest mission fields in the world.

This means we can no longer attribute what we view as missions as something that is happening "over there." It is something that must happen here. This is our mission field. We are missionaries to twenty-first-century America. We must begin to see ourselves this way if we are to be effective.

Begin to see yourself as an intentional missionary who has been sent to a land that is pagan, idolatrous, and, for the most part, has no biblical knowledge or worldview. How would you approach this mission field? You would probably want to learn the language, understand the culture, its idols, and its spiritual strongholds in order to know how to effectively engage it. This would take a deliberate mindset and engagement. It is exactly the approach each of us and our churches must take to effectively engage our culture with the gospel.

I think one of the healthiest things that every Christ follower can do to gain a greater understanding of God's heart for the nations of the world as well as our own culture is to go on a short-term missions trip to a different nation. It is there that our hearts can be expanded, and we can begin to see the veneer of our own American biases and comfort.

I personally make it a habit to go on at least one missions trip every other year to a third world nation to participate in missions work of some sort. For me it has helped me remember that our God is a global God and our mission is a global mission. It also helps keep me reminded of how blessed I really am and the responsibility I have to the poor and the powerless. Our church sends teams each year on short-term trips to serve others in the name of Jesus. I have yet to find a person who has gone on such a trip and comes back unchanged and unchallenged.

Remembering that Jesus told us that we would be witnesses beginning in Jerusalem but ultimately to the uttermost parts of the world is a perspective that will keep us healthy and motivated wherever we are (Acts 1:8). Our Jerusalem is the community we live in. It is our neighborhoods, Little Leagues our kids play in, the cubicle we work in, the hallway we walk down every day to our classes, the Starbucks we frequent every morning, and the malls we shop in. It is the gospel mission that we pass by as we drive through our downtown areas. There are so many opportunities right in our backyards that we may miss if we only think of missions as something "others" do in far off lands.

MISSION BASES

How we view our churches must change as well. If all of God's people are missionaries, and every field is a mission field, then the church buildings and organizations must begin to be viewed as mission bases. It is cliché to say that the church isn't the building but the people. But as often as this may be stated, it must be understood how important it is that the church does gather and why.

There is a recurrent movement of people who want to gather only in homes and see church buildings and gatherings as a heretical deviation from New Testament Christianity. I don't believe this could be further from the truth. While it is true that buildings and programs are not essentially necessary for the church to thrive and that Paul did not necessarily have large buildings and programs in his missionary endeavors, it is dangerous and unbiblical to abandon these tools. Paul did not have computers either, but had he had them, or the Internet, rest assured he would have used them to fulfill his ministry and calling. As in any movement there is sometimes evidence of over-adjusting due to excess or error. While I disagree with the idea that in order for the church to return to a "New Testament" order, we must abandon buildings and structures, I do embrace the fresh emphasis upon community and a reshifting back to the focus being outside the four walls of the building instead of becoming building centric.

What we need is a fresh perspective of why we gather together and how buildings and programs fit into that. Very simply put, they serve as the mission base for the efforts of the kingdom in our community. They serve as a place of training, encouragement, and a sending station. Every weekend and throughout the week believers gather to worship Jesus, to be taught the Scriptures, to be edified and built up, and to be sent out to the mission field of our culture. It is a place where our lamps are refilled with oil to keep us aflame and bright. There is something about the corporate anointing that takes place in larger gatherings that cannot be replaced with just a small-group mentality. Perhaps this is why even the apostles gathered all the believers together in Solomon's portico in the temple, beyond just meeting together house to house.

It's vital for us to view the church this way because it has become increasingly popular to see the church service as the primary means of evangelism. Attractionalism, as it is referred to, has its place in a culture that is used to "sight and sound" big production presentations. Inviting our friends and coworkers to church is a great way to introduce Jesus to the unchurched and allow the presence of God to impact their lives. The unfortunate thing is that for many believers this is the *only* sort of evangelism they will ever engage in. We should utilize every tool at our disposal, including the attractional model, to win as many to the Lord as we possibly can. But if we are relying upon the pastor to be the only witness to who Jesus is and what He has done, we are leaving behind our own responsibility to be engaged in mission. The renowned Roman Catholic theologian Hans Kung has stated it this way:

> The church least of all can be an end in itself. Everything the Church does must be directed towards fulfilling its apostolic mission to the outside world; it must minister to the world and to mankind. To be a Church and to have a mission are not two separate things. To be itself, the Church must follow the apostles in continually recognizing and demonstrating that it has been sent out to the world.[9]

A missional approach is required in each of us who views the church and its "services" as only one means of presentation of the gospel. Every believer must be equipped to share the story in their own way and in their respective places of influence. Each of us is called to pray, give, and share boldly about Jesus Christ. The church must be viewed as the mission base from which all of us are being trained and sent, and where we can return to celebrate all that He has done through each of us on the mission field.

MISSION FUEL

The place of prayer to motivate the church for its mission cannot be overstated. Prayer is the fuel oil that the church's mission engine runs on. When our tank is empty, our engine sputters to an abrupt stop. Zinzendorf and the Moravians caught fire in the furnace of prayer, and the world was changed forever. From the very beginning of the church carrying the torch of the Jesus mission in the world, prayer has been the companion compound necessary for an evangelism explosion. Jesus commanded the first followers to wait for the descent of the Holy Spirit with power, and for ten days they prayed. Critical mass was achieved when a prayerful people were doused with fire from heaven. The first signs of life from this newly birthed entity called *the church* was the prophetic proclamation of Jesus as King and the immediate conversion of thousands. One would not have happened without the other, and it still will not today.

I believe that one of the secret connections between prayer and evangelism is its constant recalibration of God's servants back to the heartbeat of Father God. Jesus lived in a constant state of inhale and exhale of secret prayer and then external ministry and demonstration. He would disappear to a desolate place of prayer with the Father and then from there minister in great power. He did all of this in obedience to God's will.

In these days he went out to the mountain to pray, and all night he continued in prayer to God. . . . And he came down with them and stood on a level place, with a great crowd of his disciples and a great multitude of people from all Judea and Jerusalem and the seacoast of Tyre and Sidon, who came to hear him and to be healed of their diseases. And those who were troubled with unclean spirits were cured. And all the crowd sought to touch him, for power came out of him and healed them all.

—LUKE 6:12, 17–19

If we are called to be followers and imitators of Jesus, then what He did and valued, we must also do and value. Jesus knew He had a very short time to accomplish His mission, and yet He prioritized time with the Father and intercessory prayer for others. It was out of this place of prevailing prayer that effectiveness and passionate motivation flowed. The first disciples followed this pattern and bore the same fruit. Dick Eastman, one of the most influential voices to the church on the subject of intercessory prayer, observes:

In no other way can the believer become as fully involved with God's work, especially the work of world evangelism, as in intercessory prayer.[10]

Once when Charles Spurgeon—the prince of preachers—was asked by a visiting minister what the key to his success was, he led the guest down to the basement through long hallways to a small, obscure room. Upon opening the door, he pointed to a group of intercessory warriors who were praying with fervent intensity. The revivalist is noted as saying, "This is the engine room of the church. Without prayer my words fall to the ground."

We need a prayer revolution in the American church. We need a return to heartfelt intercession for the lost in our cities and the nations of the world. There are many great churches that are modeling this and seeing God do the miraculous in their midst. They are experiencing a renewed passion for the cause of the slain Lamb of God coming to a boil. Whole movements are renewing their commitment to unceasing prayer around the clock for the evangelism of the world and spiritual breakthroughs to occur in our hardhearted, apathetic culture.

C. T. Studd, the famous missionary from England, once said, "The light that shines farthest shines brightest at home." The secret place of prayer is the rightful home of every Christian and every church. Our passion for Jesus will shine no farther into the darkness of this world than it does in our pursuit of loving God and hearing His voice in prayer. If we are going to overcome the climate of apathy and spiritual atrophy, prevailing prayer will become our new norm and greatest addiction.

Conclusion

DIMMERS AND LAMPSHADES

Ask of Me, and I will give you the nations for your inheritance, and the ends of the earth as your possession.

—PSALM 2:8, NKJV

MAGINE WITH ME what would, could, and should happen if the church renewed its devotion to the Upper Room from whence we came. Heaven does not turn a deaf ear to the cries of its citizens as they seek, knock, and ask.

This is our inheritance, and this is our mission: to be the light to the world that gives off the colors of His goodness and dispels the darkness that blinds this world from the One who loves them and gave Himself for them, to shine the light of His glory as we come from the place of prayer as Jesus did from the Mount of Transfiguration and as Moses did when he came down from Sinai, radiating His presence to all those who are watching us. We are called to take our stand, the lamp stand that God has fashioned uniquely for each of us to shine brightly.

OK, so we know all of this. We have experienced God's love and grace in our lives. We have been brought out of darkness and into the light. We have heard all of the sermons and sung all the songs. We know the need and even felt the burden at times. What in the world would keep us from rising up with faith in our hearts to be all God created us to be and do all God purposed for us to do? What are those "things" that keep the church from shining as brightly or as intentionally as we should function as lampshades and

209

dimmers? They are methods that the enemy uses in his volatile desperation to keep the church hardly visible or distinguishable. They are subtle trappings to dial us down and cover us up. Jesus said, "Nor do people light a lamp and put it under a basket" (Matt. 5:15). In other words, you were not created to be covered up. You were created and re-created to stand up and stand out. You are not a secret to be kept but a beacon to expose the truth. The devil will do everything he can to keep you and me and the churches that we belong to from doing what should come most natural to us—shine!

The list of these instruments is long—intimidation, compromise, fear, doubt, unbelief, procrastination, division, greed, distraction, depression, busyness, hatred, apathy, selfishness, persecution, deception, and the list goes on and on. The only light this world will ever see is the light we choose to give. If we allow the enemy to keep us under cover, the world will remain in darkness, and we will pass on to the next generation the next Dark Age.

It's time to take the lampshades off and flip the switch on the dimmer to full tilt! It's time to change out our soft light sixty-watt bulbs for floodlights and turn on every light in the house. The world is waiting and watching, and heaven is too. Crowded around the banister of heaven are all those who have gone on before us and served their generations well, setting the stage for this moment in history. The men and women who are watching faithfully served, prayed, were persecuted unto death, hated in their own lifetime, and laid the groundwork upon which you and I are building. They are cheering for us—this great cloud of witnesses. They have seen and continue to behold the face of Jesus. They can see the finish line of God's redemptive plan in sight. Can you hear them? They are echoing what they hear the voice of God saying to you and me, "Arise, shine, for your light has come, and the glory of the LORD has risen upon you" (Isa. 60:1).

If we could see this as clearly as they see it, we would not shrink back. We would be astounded at the glory of God upon us and the favor of God toward us. We would see prophetically the nations coming to Jesus and the church elevated as a house of hope and storehouse of salvation. The false identity we have been living under would disintegrate before us, and we would square our shoulders back and put our hand to the plow with a holy adrenaline rush. In the words of the prophet Isaiah, we would *see all around us, and our hearts would swell with joy* (Isa. 60:5).

This is my prayer for each of us. This is my commitment to my generation: to lead us to this place of understanding and revelation and to call a generation to push back the darkness and *be radiant!*

May God be pleased with how brightly we shine.

NOTES

CHAPTER 1
Arise, Shine

1. Frank Peretti, *This Present Darkness* (Wheaton, IL: Crossway Books, 1986).

CHAPTER 2
Enter the Void

1. As quoted in Mark Batterson, *Wild Goose Chase* (Colorado Springs, CO: Multnomah Books, 2008), 149. Viewed at Google Books.

2. BrainyQuote, "Martin Luther King, Jr. Quotes," http:// www.brainyquote.com/quotes/quotes/m/martinluth101472.html (accessed October 25, 2012).

3. Howard Robinson, "Dualism," *The Stanford Encyclopedia of Philosophy (Winter 2011 Edition)*, Edward N. Zalta, ed., http:// plato.stanford.edu/archives/win2011/entries/dualism/ (accessed October 25, 2012).

CHAPTER 3
The Power of One Light

1. ActiveWater, "Our Core Values," http://www.activewater.org/ index.php?pr=Our_Core_Values (accessed October 25, 2012).

2. As told to the author by Daren Wendell in July 2012.

3. C. S. Lewis, *The Lion, the Witch and the Wardrobe* (New York: HarperCollins Publishers, 2004), 194. Viewed at Google Books.

4. Marcus Tillius Cicero, *The Orations of Marcus Tullius Cicero*, trans. C. D. Younge (London: H.G. Bohn, 1956), 4:6.

5. Richard A. Batey, *Jesus and the Forgotten City: New Light on Sepphoris and the Urban World of Jesus* (n.p.: CenturyOne Media, 2000).

6. BiblePlaces.com, "Sepphoris," http://www.bibleplaces.com/ sepphoris.htm (accessed October 29, 2012).

7. Rick Renner, "Lift Your Light Higher and Increase Your Influence in the World," Impart, http://impartnow.org/ wordpress/?p=758 (accessed October 29, 2012).

CHAPTER 4
Color Your World

1. "Inside" by Jared Anderson. Copyright © 2009 Don Quixote Publishing Integrity Worship Music. Permission requested.
2. Brain Zahnd, *Beauty Will Save the World* (Lake Mary, FL: Charisma House, 2012), 215.

CHAPTER 5
People From the Future

1. *The Matrix*, directed by Andy Wachowski and Larry Wachowski (Burbank, CA: Warner Bros., 1999), DVD.
2. N. T. Wright, "The Uncomfortable Truth of Easter," a sermon at the Sung Eucharist in Durham Cathedral, Easter 2008, http://ntwrightpage.com/sermons/EasterDay08.htm (accessed October 29, 2012).
3. George Ladd, *The Presence of the Future* (Grand Rapids, MI: Wm. B. Eerdmans Publishing Co., 1974), 225.
4. Eugene Peterson, *Practice Resurrection* (Grand Rapids, MI: Wm. B. Eerdmans Publishing Co., 2010), 12.
5. N. T. Wright, *After You Believe* (New York: HarperCollins Publishers, 2010), 137. Viewed at Google Books.
6. *Back to the Future*, directed by Robert Zemeckis (Universal City, CA: Amblin Entertainment, 1985).
7. Eugene H. Peterson, *The Pastor* (New York: HarperCollins Publishers, 2011), 110.
8. Stanley Hauerwas, *Resident Aliens* (Nashville: Abingdon Press, 1989), 92.
9. Walter A. Elwell and Philip W. Comfort, eds., *Tyndale Bible Dictionary* (Carol Stream, IL: Tyndale House Publishers, Inc., 2001).

CHAPTER 6
BE Word Centered: In Shifting Times

1. A. W. Tozer, *The Pursuit of God* (n.p.: Wilder Publications, 2008), 9. Viewed at Google Books.
2. Martin Davies, *The Gutenberg Bible* (London: The British Library, 1996).
3. David Dewey, *A User's Guide to Bible Translations* (Downers Grove, IL: InterVarsity Press, 2004). Viewed at Google Books.

4. Daniel Radosh, "The Good Book Business," *The New Yorker*, December 18, 2006, http://www.newyorker.com/ archive/2006/12/18/061218fa_fact1 (accessed October 29, 2012).

5. Frank Newport, "One-Third of Americans Believe the Bible Is Literally True," GALLUP, May 25, 2007, gallup.com/poll/27682/ onethird-americans-believe-bible-literally-true.aspx (accessed November 19, 2012).

6. Mark Batterson, *Primal* (Colorado Springs, CO: Multnomah Books, 2009), 169. Viewed at Google Books.

7. N. T. Wright, *Simply Christian* (New York: HarperCollins Publishers, 2006), 182–183. Viewd at Google Books.

CHAPTER 7
BE Spirit Filled: In a World Running on Empty

1. Francis Chan, *Forgotten God* (Colorado Springs, CO: David C. Cook Publishing, 2009), 32. Viewed at Google Books.

2. A.W. Tozer, *Life in the Spirit* (Peabody, MA: Hendrickson Publishers,2009), 72. Viewed at Google Books.

3. Jack Hayford, *Living the Spirit-Formed Life* (Ventura, CA: Regal Books, 2001), 118. Viewed at Google Books.

CHAPTER 8
BE People Oriented: In a Self-Centered Society

1. Thinkexist.com, "Mother Teresa Quotes," http://thinkexist .com/quotation/being-unwanted-unloved-uncared-for-forgotten -by/530665.html (accessed November 21, 2012).

2. David Kinnaman, *Unchristian* (Grand Rapids, MI: Baker Books, 2007), 212–213. Viewed at Google Books.

3. Seth Godin, *Tribes* (New York: Penguin Group (USA) Inc., 2008).

CHAPTER 9
BE Kingdom Focused: In a Spiritually Blinded Culture

1. Frederick Buechner, *Listening to Your Life* (New York: Harper Collins Publishers, 1992).

2. See 1 Samuel 5, a reference to the idol of the Philistines being found on its face before the captured Ark of the Lord.

3. Chaim Potok, *Wanderings: Chaim Potok's History of the Jews* (New York: Random House, Inc., 1978).

4. Bob Hamp, *Think Differently, Live Differently* (n.p.: Thinking Differently Press, 2010), 182

5. *The Matrix*, directed by Andy Wachowski and Larry Wachowski.

6. Eugene Peterson, *The Jesus Way* (Grand Rapids: Wm. B. Eerdmans Publishing Co., 2007), 22.

7. Wright, *After You Believe*, 105. Viewed at Google Books.

CHAPTER 10
BE Mission Motivated: In a Climate of Apathy

1. As quoted in Marcia Ford *Traditions of the Ancients* (Nashville: Broadman and Holman Publishers, 2006), 99. Viewed at Google Books.

2. FinestQuotes.com, "Missionaries Quotes," http://www .finestquotes.com/select_quote-category-Missionaries-page-2.htm (accessed October 30, 2012).

3. John R. Weinlick, *Count Zinzendorf* (New York and Nashville: Abingdon Press, 1956).

4. Felix Bovet, *Count Zinzendorf* (Hampton, TN: Harvey & Tait Publishing, 2000), 36.

5. A. J. Lewis, *Zinzendorf: The Ecumenical Pioneer* (London: SCM Press Ltd., 1962), 59.

6. Awake and Go Global Prayers Network, "Count Zinzendorf and the Moravians," http://www.watchword.org/index .php?option=com_content&task=view&id=48&Itemid=48 (accessed October 30, 2012).

7. As quoted in Ann Dunagan *The Mission-Minded Child* (Colorado Springs, CO: Authentic Publishing, 2007), 81. Viewed at Google Books.

8. Harvest Ministry, "100 Mission Mottos (& Missionary Quotes)," http://harvestministry.org/100-mission-mottos (accessed October 30, 2012).

9. As quoted in Larry Caldwell, *Sent Out! Reclaiming the Spiritual Gift of Apostleship for Missionaries and Churches Today.* (Pasadena, CA: William Carey Library, 1992), 133.

10. Dick Eastman, *The Hour That Changes the World* (Grand Rapids, MI: Chosen Books, 2002), 72. Viewed at Google Books.

ABOUT THE AUTHOR

Lee Cummings is the founding and lead pastor of Radiant Church, a thriving, Spirit-empowered, evangelical church in Kalamazoo, Michigan. Lee is also the president of the Resurrection Life Churches International (RLCI) family of churches based in Grand Rapids, Michigan. He and his wife, Jane, have been married for twenty years and have three teenage children—Ashley, Jared, and Tiffany. Lee is a sought-after speaker for conferences and churches and an emerging voice to the twenty-first-century church. For more information about Lee or Radiant Church, you may visit radiantchurch.tv, download the app "Be Radiant" for iPhone or Droid, and follow him on Twitter @Lee_cummings.

PASSIO

PASSIONATE. AUTHENTIC. MISSIONAL.

Passio brings you books, e-books, and other media from innovative voices on topics from missional living **to a deeper relationship with God.**

TAKE A LOOK AT PASSIO'S OTHER RELEASES
at the links below and ignite your faith and spiritual passion.

www.passiofaith.com
www.twitter.com/passiofaith
www.facebook.com/passiofaith

11299C